PARRY
THOMAS

PARRY THOMAS

THE FIRST DRIVER TO BE KILLED IN
PURSUIT OF THE LAND SPEED RECORD

Hugh Tours

PEN & SWORD
TRANSPORT

PARRY THOMAS
The First Driver to be Killed in Pursuit of the Land Speed Record

This edition published in 2019 by Pen & Sword Transport,
an imprint of Pen & Sword Books Ltd,
47 Church Street, Barnsley, S. Yorkshire, S70 2AS

First published as *Parry Thomas: Designer-Driver* by B.T. Batsford Ltd., 1959.

Typeset in 11.5/16 point Palatino by Dave Cassan.
Printed and bound by TJ International Ltd, Padstow, Cornwall

Pen & Sword Books Ltd incorporates the imprints of Frontline Books, Pen &
Sword Archaeology, Air World Books, Atlas, Aviation, Battleground, Discovery,
Family History, History, Maritime, Military, Naval, Politics, Social History, True
Crime, Claymore Press, Frontline Books, Praetorian Press, Seaforth Publishing
and White Owl

For a complete list of Pen & Sword titles please contact:

PEN & SWORD BOOKS LTD
47 Church Street, Barnsley, South Yorkshire, S70 2AS, UK.
E-mail: enquiries@pen-and-sword.co.uk
Website: www.pen-and-sword.co.uk

Or

PEN AND SWORD BOOKS,
1950 Lawrence Roadd, Havertown, PA 19083, USA
E-mail: Uspen-and-sword@casematepublishers.com
Website: www.penandswordbooks.com

Contents

Foreword

by Sir Henry Spurrier

Chairman and Managing Director of Leyland Motors Ltd.

From the time I was a schoolboy before World War I, Parry Thomas was almost one of the family. Associated with my father in many engineering problems, they had become close friends. More than this, however, he had endeared himself to the younger element, and become very definitely an admired member of our circle. He coached us at cricket and tennis, being himself a no mean performer at both sports. In fact, I am sure, if he could have spared himself the time, he would have attained a high standard as a tennis player. Throughout his life he was the hero and friend of all the young people he knew.

In the few years left to him after the War, I was to know him as the brilliant engineer, and it is particularly to that period I wish to refer. I lost sight of him during the War, but we came together again in 1919; he had been appointed Chief Engineer of Leyland Motors Limited, and I returned to continue my training. He was working on the development of a very advanced design of aircraft engine, and also on the famous Leyland eight-cylinder car. Reid Railton, by then demobbed from the R.N.V.R., had joined Parry Thomas as his assistant designer. About that time Leyland decided to stop further work on the aero engine and concentrate all energies on the car, which was completed and shown at the Olympia Motor Show in 1920, where it took the public by storm and was referred to as "The Lion of Olympia".

Parry Thomas's history and all he did is told to you in the pages of this book. In this foreword I wish to confine my few words to the memories I have of him as Parry Thomas the man. Before all, I remember him as a Welshman with a dynamic and arresting personality, intolerant, of course, as are all good engineers, probably the most brilliant inventor of his day, and kind and generous, with a helping hand for anyone in need. He was godfather to our elder daughter, whom he spoilt as he would have done any child of his own.

When the slump in the early '20s hit Leyland Motors very hard, with reluctance it was decided that production of the car would have to be discontinued. Parry Thomas by that time had begun to make a name for himself as a racing driver of outstanding ability. He had put his heart wholly into the new car, and could not bear to see his new creation relegated to the scrapheap. He decided to take a big chance, to leave Leyland, and take all that was left of the "Eight" production, and begin a racing career.

Parry Thomas's friendship with me and my family continued as before until the time of his death. To-day, over thirty years later, my memory of him is as vivid as ever. To me he will always be a hero and the finest automobile engineer I have ever known.

HENRY SPURRIER

Rhodesia, April 1959

Acknowledgement

In accumulating material for this book, I have been greatly helped by the kindness of many people who have so willingly cast back their thoughts to a period over thirty years ago and who have allowed me to question them unmercifully. I want to thank them all.

In particular, I would like to acknowledge the help I have received from members of the Thomas family, Mr. and Mrs. Geoffrey Thomas and Mr. D.J. Hickman, and from the late J.G. Parry Thomas's friends, Mr. Reid Railton, Mr. Kenneth Taylor and Major L.G. Callingham. I am most grateful to Sir Henry Spurrier for contributing his Foreword, and to Mr. A.B. Chadwick, Publicity Manager of Leyland Motors Ltd., who accorded me every facility that I could wish for, while Mr. A. Bourne, Director of Messrs. Iliffe and Sons, Ltd., kindly permitted me to search through the files of *The Autocar*. Mr. William Boddy, Editor of *Motor Sport*, who, I understand, had thought of writing about Thomas himself, very generously put his knowledge at my disposal. The Editors of *The Autocar*, *The Motor* and *The Automobile Engineer* have also had the kindness to allow me to quote from their journals.

I would like to thank, too, Mr. R.C. Porter for his enthusiastic encouragement and for his useful notes on the Thomas

Transmission, and Mr. Anthony Harding, of Batsford's, for the invaluable assistance without which this book would never have been produced.

Others who have been extremely helpful, though I regret that space permits me only to mention their names, are: Mr. Harold Parker, Mr. and Mrs. T. Wisdom, Mr. J. Eason Gibson, Mr. Peter Garnier, Miss M.E. Hillock, Mr. P. Edwards, Mr. Newton Iddon, Capt. A. Frazer-Nash, Mr. A. Braid, Mr. Ian Clark, Mr. P. Craven, Mr. C. Durlacher, Mr. Wilfred Morgan, Mr. Johns and Mrs. Joan Simpson.

Autumn, 1959
H.T.

The Author and the Publishers are grateful to the following for their permission to reproduce the illustrations in this book:

The Editor of *The Autocar*, for figs. 10, 12, 14, 15, 18, 19, 22, 24, 28 and 29; The Editor of *The Automobile Engineer*, for fig. 5; Barratt's Photo Press Ltd., for fig. 30; Mr. Anthony Brittan, for fig. 21; Mr. W.J. Brunell, for fig. 17; Fox Photos. Ltd., for fig. 32; *Radio Times* Hulton Picture Library, for figs. 2, 13, 16 and 31; Leyland Motors Ltd., for figs. 6-9 and 11; London News Agency Ltd., for fig. 33; Mr. Kenneth Taylor, for fig. 27; Temple Press Ltd., for fig. 1; Topical Press Agency Ltd., for figs. 4, 23, 25, 26 and 34; the Editor *of Sports Cars Illustrated*, for fig. 20; Sport and General Press Agency Ltd., for figs. 3, 35 and 36.

The diagram on page 146 was redrawn by Mr. Dennis Marshall, A.R.I.B.A.

List of Illustrations

The numerals in parentheses in the text refer to the *figure numbers* of illustrations.

Figure

CHAPTER I

The Personal Angle

For a man who avoided any unnecessary publicity, the passing of over thirty years since his tragic and untimely death is sufficient to justify the assumption that many of the present generation of motor racing enthusiasts have not even heard of the name of Parry Thomas. It will be appropriate therefore, even if a little unorthodox, to start by quoting in full the obituary notice which appeared in the house journal of Leyland Motors Ltd. It met with the approval of the men who worked with him, knew him and admired him and it has, in consequence, an authenticity which is unchallengeable. It begins:

Chief Engineer John Godfrey Parry Thomas was always just plain Thomas to those of us who worked and played alongside him at Leyland from February 1917 to 31st December 1923. The tragedy of the Pendine Sands let loose a flood of reminiscences in the daily and the motor press and not a few of the scribes hastened to record that they had known "Tommy" intimately and personally. None of us at Leyland knew him as intimately as that, and we take leave to doubt if, at the most, more than one or two of his closest friends ever felt near enough in addressing the real man to venture such a personality. Thomas was a very shy fellow, he clearly discouraged intimacy, he disliked hero-worship

1

and blatant publicity. He could have had a surfeit of them both in his Brooklands years. He was diffident of praise, very proud, but very modest. He could be angry. When worried or baulked, he could at times be irritable. But the deep kindliness of his nature brought him almost at once with an apology or a proffered handshake to one whom he may have felt he had hurt.

Have you ever before seen his signature? Unknowing, you would not have deciphered it. Those who claim to see character in calligraphy would have no difficulty in diagnosing from it the quick brain in advance of the sure hand, impatience with routine, but little use for compromise, distaste for delay and a hundred per cent sense of direction.

Than "J.G.P.T." none of us have known a greater engineering-sportsman – there have been many driver-sportsmen, amateur mechanic-drivers, great steersmen, but never a finer combination than the man whose going has left us with such a sense of personal loss. Thomas always played a straight bat, drove a straight course. A fine cricketer and a more than average tennis player. He danced well, and while generally bothering little as to his personal appearance, on occasion could turn out as immaculate as a Guardsman for some festive gathering.

His brilliant technical skill, his personal strength and athleticism, his amazing nerve and pluck, his nervous and gentle temperament, his inbred courtesy, his high sense of honour, even his moods of abstraction, all these endeared him to us as a colleague and a comrade. But has anything quite brought the lump into our throats like the news of the carefully concealed endowments of cots for poor and sick kiddies? We knew that side of bachelor Thomas' character – but we never suspected its depth. A wonderful and most pathetic character lost to all of us!

In his use of the word "pathetic" with its meaning of "moving, stirring and affecting" the writer of the above has put his finger on the pulse of the whole story of Thomas's life.

Born in Wrexham, on 6th April 1885, where his father, the Rev. J.W. Thomas, was curate, Godfrey was a second son; his brother Geoffrey being his senior by two years. He would have remembered little, if anything, of the town of his birth, for in January 1888, when he was not quite three years old, his father was appointed vicar of Bwlch-y-Cibau, a quietly delightful Montgomeryshire village. Here, in a comfortable, creeper-covered vicarage, the family lived for sixteen years – a family which increased by the addition of three daughters, Mollie, Madge and Joyce.

The young Parry Thomas must have enjoyed a most pleasant childhood in this Welsh village centred round the little church, designed by Sir Gilbert Scott, where his father was a popular figure among his parishioners. He was fond of his sisters, who were to grow up into pretty women, and they were, no doubt, a great asset when it came to the arranging of parties, dances or picnics. His mother was rather an imperious woman who commanded respect more than devotion from her children. Before she was married she was a Parry, hence Thomas's third name, and her family, far back, was connected with that fearsome character in history, Judge Jeffreys. Godfrey was her special favourite, and although she disapproved of his wanting to take up engineering as a career and felt that the Army or the Church was a far more suitable calling for a son of hers, she did nothing to curb his enthusiasm. In fact, she assisted him financially during his early years as an engineer. Spiritualism played a considerable part in her life, and it was doubtless the shock of Thomas's death that increased this trait and caused her to arrange a seance at "The Hermitage" at Brooklands, in an endeavour to make contact with her son. The results, as far as can be ascertained, were quite negative.

Mr. Reid Railton has said that Thomas was a master of original thought. He was, of course, referring to the ingenuities of Thomas's mind at a much later period, but the seeds were unquestionably germinating in the brain of the schoolboy when, at Oswestry School, he thought up the idea of raffling his sixpence-a-week pocket money at a penny a chance to as many takers as he could find.

At the age of seventeen he started his career by taking a course of electrical engineering at the City and Guilds Engineering College in London, and it was here, incidentally, that he met Kenneth Thomson, a New Zealander, who was to become his intimate friend and assistant during the Brooklands period of his life. At the end of the course he spent some months in research work on induction motors under the late Professor Ayrton. Then, from 1905 to 1907, he worked as an apprentice, gaining experience in the shops of Siemens Brothers & Co. Ltd., and later in those of Clayton and Shuttleworth Ltd.

By the end of 1907, at the age of twenty-two, he had set up on his own, helped, no doubt, by pecuniary assistance from his mother, and was experimenting privately on an electrical transmission for motor vehicles. The results showed a promise of success and attracted the attention of Kenneth Thomson's brother, Hedley Thomson, who, with a Mr. W.F. Hickman, put up sufficient funds for the formation of two companies – Thomas Transmission Ltd. and Thomas Foreign Patents Ltd. – of which Thomas himself was a joint managing director. The Thomas

Transmission, which is the subject of the following chapter, was developed and adapted during the next four years.

Thomas, who had previously owned several motorcycles including a 350-c.c. Kerry with which he made the fastest time of the day at a meeting organised by the Central Technical College, South Kensington, at Brockley Hill in 1905, now owned a Belgian Pipe car to which he had fitted Thomas transmission. A second Pipe, similarly modified, was used for demonstrations, and Mr. Hickman's Delahaye was also converted and ran with considerable success.

It was at this time that Thomas's associations with Leyland Motors Ltd. commenced. With offices first in Kensington High Street and later on at No. 29 Spring Gardens, which were to be his to the very end, Thomas required workshop facilities for work of a fairly heavy nature. Leylands, as the largest manufacturers of lorries, were approached and arrangements were made with Mr. Henry Spurrier for part of one of their bays to be available for Thomas's use; Leyland mechanics and fitters being hired as and when they were wanted. The electrical work which could not be done at Leylands was carried out by arrangement with Dick Kerr Ltd. of Preston.

Henry Spurrier, junior (now Sir Henry Spurrier), whose father was then general manager, became closely acquainted with Thomas at this stage, and a great deal of both work and leisure time was spent in each other's company. Thus, began the long association between the names of Leyland and Thomas.

By 1914, the Thomas Transmission had had its day. It was not, it seems, the advent of the war that spoilt its chances but rather the fact that, although workable and efficient, the transmission proved too expensive to be a practical proposition – at any rate, at that time.

During the war Thomas's services were utilised by the Government in an advisory capacity, mostly to do with the development of aero engines, although 1917 found him sitting on a commission concerning itself with the design of tanks. He had also given thought to the propulsion of airships and had evolved a system of electrical transmission for this purpose. Briefly, it consisted of a central power plant incorporating a generator which drove as many propellers as were required by means of electric motors situated with their respective propellers at the end of outriggers from the main frame of the airship. Only one experimental electric motor was actually produced (by Dick Kerr Ltd.) for this scheme and was subsequently used for many years by Leylands for the brake testing of their engines.

In 1917, Thomas returned to Leylands, but this time it was in the capacity of Chief Engineer. His first job was to be the development of an eighteen-cylinder aero engine designed by the former Chief Engineer, a Scotsman named Ferguson. Thomas soon put this to one side and produced an eight-cylinder aircraft engine of his own (6). It had four banks of two cylinders in X formation. The blocks were of aluminium with wet liners, and each of the four cylinder heads carried an overhead camshaft operating valves controlled by leaf springs. The whole engine, developing 350 b.h.p., was light enough for two men to lift. By August 1918 it was ready for Air Ministry type testing but, most unfortunately, the Government representatives arrived a fortnight before they were expected. The prototype engine was hurriedly assembled and run up on test. Not surprisingly, it seized. But now that the war was over the Air Ministry gradually lost interest in such engines. Leylands saw no future in continuing with the project and so it was dropped. It is perhaps interesting to note, however, that in 1929, when the Air Ministry issued a review of ten years of aero engine design, the Thomas-designed Leyland engine was second on their list.

From conversations with men who had worked at Leylands during Thomas's time, it is evident that he found his life both full and satisfying. He was absorbed in the design of a car of magnificent proportions without the frustration of having to keep down the cost. Few men of genius in the engineering industry have ever had quite such a free rein. But this did not go to his head, and he found time to take considerable interest in the welfare of those working under him. It is said that his journeys around the workshops, however urgent, were inevitably held up while he chatted with some employee, asking after his family, his rheumatism or some such personal matter. Had it been that he did this to ingratiate himself with the hands or to patronise them, the deceit would quickly have been discovered by the type of man with whom he was dealing. Instead, they recognised generosity and kind-heartedness when they saw it, and Thomas's name, even to this day, is greeted at Leylands with a smile and a look in the eye that is difficult to describe.

He could certainly lose his temper, a state which was accompanied by a particularly malicious grin and one which was caused as often as not by the foolish comment that something was "good enough". At the same time, he was very long suffering when it became apparent that a workman did not understand his instructions. Calmly and in the most friendly manner on these occasions he would explain all over again, and in the simplest language, exactly what it was that he wanted.

His love of children was an enduring characteristic throughout his life and, of course, much publicised in the press after his death when his secret donations to the Great Ormond Street Hospital and the Belgrave Hospital for Children were made known. It appeared that he had visited Great Ormond Street – introducing himself as "Mr. Thomas, an engineer" – and had enquired how much it would cost to endow a cot for a year. On being told that the figure was £50, he paid £25 down and promised the remainder in a few weeks. It subsequently came to light that the first sum represented his fee for a B.B.C. broadcast while the rest was a payment made to him by Selfridges for the privilege of exhibiting "Babs" after it had broken the world's land speed record.

On the staff sports days at Leylands, it was always Thomas who organised the children's races and who insisted on personally buying all the toys needed for prizes.

One can only guess at the reasons why children had such a fascination for him. In the first place, the fact that he was a large and powerful man himself, with a definite streak of kind-hearted sentiment in his character, would accentuate the obvious appeal of the young. Secondly, his honesty and straightforwardness, which were, perhaps, the greatest reasons for his own universal popularity, would make distasteful the less attractive traits which adults are so prone to develop. It would be quite true to say that he never suffered fools gladly, but it is also true that, in a general way, children are not fools. In his years of fame when his cars were exhibited at the Schoolboys' Exhibition, he was regularly in attendance and was delighted to encourage the young idea. But small boys can be singularly unattractive on occasion and Thomas's good nature had its limits, as was instanced by the occasion at a motor show when he announced that he was only signing autographs that day for little girls and rigidly kept to his decision. Latterly, when he was staying at the Beach Hotel, Pendine, during record attempts, it was the children of Mr. Ebsworth, the proprietor, who saw most of Thomas during the evenings.

It goes almost without saying that he was also fond of animals, and his two devoted companions at the bungalow in Brooklands track were his Alsatians, Togo and Bess. It is said, possibly with some truth, that one of these animals became unnaturally disturbed on that fatal 3rd March before the sad news had reached "The Hermitage" and could not be quieted for several days.

As befitted an energetic man, Thomas was fond of games. He was an enthusiastic soccer player, and cricket, whether it was the sort played on the sands with his young nephews or the more serious variety when he was included in the Leyland Motors side, always found him ready to participate. Tennis attracted him too. He belonged to Queen's Club during his years at Brooklands; a fact which persuaded the press to refer to him as an expert player. Mrs. Satterthwaite, famous at Wimbledon in her day, remembers playing in matches with him at Craigside, near Llandudno, and is therefore a more reliable critic of his form. She recollects that he had a charming personality and that he was excellent company but, in her own words, "Poor dear, he wasn't much good as a player."

Appearing at Brooklands meetings and breaking record after record in between whiles gave Thomas little time for anything except his work and his cars. He had no time at all for the journalists seeking interviews. To them he appeared a heavy giant of a man, inevitably dressed in old flannel trousers and a worn Fair Isle pullover, whose bulldog jowl and apparently sullen expression offered no compensations for the lack of attention they received. They therefore made their own erroneous judgements and printed fables which referred to him as a misogynist. To them and their readers he became the "Hermit of Brooklands" or "Dare-devil Thomas" who would not touch women with a barge pole. How wrong they were, and how Thomas must have smiled as he read their articles. While it would be quite true to say that his all-engrossing last love was named "Babs" and ran on four wheels, he had throughout his life been extremely fond of women, and women, such was his charm, had been extremely fond of him. The fact that his private life has remained private to this day is a great credit to him and the most gentlemanly gesture that could have been made to the ladies of his close acquaintance.

Thomas's skill as a designer amounted to genius, and a great many of his ideas were ahead of their time. The reason why he was not more famous than he was, and why he was not quite as successful as he might have been, was that he had one failing, and an easily understandable one in a man of his capabilities, which was that he was inclined to pass too little of the development work on to his draughtsmen and assistants. The 1½-litre straight-eight Thomas Special, for instance, suffered in this respect. Much that he did, however, was undoubtedly successful. The Leyland Eight, finances apart, was a magnificent car by any standards, while the Hooker-Thomas engine and the Thomas transmission were, each in their way, achievements of no little value. It is not widely known, perhaps, that the vacuum-servo brake that Thomas designed for the Leyland was eventually bought by the Dewandre Company, or that he was responsible for a type of self-locking nut (known as the "Evertite") the plans for the production of which faded away as a result of his death.

But quite apart from his engineering feats and his incredible skill as a racing driver on the track, there is one feature about John Godfrey Parry Thomas that, of itself, places him high in the ranks of men, no matter in what walk of life. No one of the very many people with whom he came into contact during his life, from the postmistress of Bwlch-y-Cibau to his intimate friends such as Mr. Reid Railton, Mr. Kenneth Taylor or Sir Henry Spurrier, has anything to say of him that does not redound to his credit as a great man and a fine sportsman.

Mr. Railton has very kindly summarised his recollections of Thomas as follows:

"No book about Thomas would be complete without some picture of the man himself, both as an individual and as an engineer. I was lucky enough to be closely associated with him as his assistant during the several years that he was with Leyland Motors Ltd., first as experimental engineer and later as chief engineer of that company. Despite the always clearly defined relationship of master and man, we became great friends. When we both left Leyland in 1923 our ways became separated, but, by then, my admiration for the man, and my interest in his activities were such that I was constantly finding my way down to Brooklands, and imposing myself on his hospitality at his bungalow inside the track. There we would sit up half the night, discussing his plans for new racing cars, in much the same way as we had talked over the design of the Leyland Eight at our digs in Preston. I am proud to say that this personal contact continued almost unbroken up until the tragic end in 1927. I offer no apology for obtruding this personal note. I do it because I think I can best depict the personality of the man by describing its impact upon myself.

Thomas (I never permitted myself the familiarity of calling him anything else. Most of his later friends among the racing fraternity called him 'Tommy', and to his family he was Godfrey. Nobody ever called him Parry) – Thomas, then, remains in my memory as by far the greatest *original thinker* that I have ever met. I never had the good fortune to know Sir Henry Royce, but, from what I have heard from his associates, I should guess that his special genius was of the same kind as Thomas's, although the men themselves could hardly have been more different. By 'original thinker' I mean an outstanding ability to arrive at a sound solution of a new problem by the logical application of first principles. Thomas's versatility in this field was amazing. His electro-mechanical 'Thomas Transmission', designed nearly fifty years ago, broke what was then completely new ground, and yet remains to-day about the neatest solution of its particular problem that has so far appeared. Then, as now, its drawbacks were those of weight and cost, but, even today, engineers in this field keep on coming back to it, and wondering whether to try it again with modern materials. The Leyland Eight car, probably his best-known production, was another example. It positively bristled with novel and logical solutions of problems which were then facing all motor car designers. Some of these solutions, unheard of at the time, are commonplace today. Torsion springs, anti-roll bars, vacuum-assisted brakes, for instance, all originated on the Leyland Eight.

As I have indicated above, he was always ready to talk over his ideas while they were germinating in his brain, in fact verbal discussion appeared to help him. It is most rare for an engineer to be both able and willing to put into words the mental processes whereby he reaches his conclusions, and to listen to him doing it was a liberal education. It is no exaggeration to say that he taught me *how to think*, and such ability as I have as an engineer I owe entirely to his teaching.

This peculiar genius of his overflowed in many different directions, but was always channelled towards the problems of the particular subject upon which he happened to be working at the time. He never indulged in the greedy dreams of the professional inventor, and, like most engineers, he hated to be called one. Engineers regard inventors much as mathematicians regard accountants. To both it is primarily the means and not the end which is important. Thomas's strength lay in his ability to find the theoretically perfect solution to the problem in hand. His weakness appeared when it became a question of how that solution should be translated into a piece of machinery. Perhaps it is hardly fair to call this a weakness. The original thinker is seldom a good machine designer, and Thomas was no exception. The best engineering management will seldom allow these two functions to be doubled in one person, but Thomas was a man of such strong personality, and such decided opinions, that it was difficult to get him to delegate detail design work that would sometimes have been better done by others. In his last years, when he had his own establishment at Brooklands, his resources were naturally limited, and this handicap became pronounced to the point where some of his brain-children did rather less than justice to the brilliant mind which had conceived them.

An interesting comparative study could be made of the widely different ways in which successful designers go to work. Some sweat it out, line by line, on the drawing board; others do all their preliminary work with freehand sketches, while a third school have the knack of doing the whole thing in their heads. Thomas belonged to the last class. He would sit for hours, staring into space, moving now and then to use his slide-rule, and occasionally to make a note on a piece of paper. It made no difference to him where he happened to be, and this occasionally had its funny side. I have seen him in the front row at a theatre, at the hushed climax of the play, suddenly pull out a slide-rule and work it vigorously. He had slightly prominent front teeth which, in relaxed moments, gave him a rather sinister grin. Strangers, particularly in railway carriages, mistaking this for a friendly smile, would sometimes respond in kind. The total absence of any reaction, coupled with the persistence of the smile, was enough to shake the strongest nerve. Having once got the conception clear in his mind, he would call in his draughtsman and give him a long verbal description of what he wanted laid out. This would often be accompanied by a few ill-executed sketches, but his exposition was so clear and explicit, that anyone used to his methods could quickly produce what he wanted. During the whole time that I knew him, I never saw him put pencil to paper on the drawing board himself.

I don't think that anyone who came under the influence of his very strong personality will ever forget it. Upon any subject which he had at heart he was a most articulate and persuasive talker. He had the valuable knack of persuading others of the feasibility of any project in which he was interested, and furthermore of convincing them that he could carry it through. He was the supreme example of Samuel Butler's dictum that the greatness of a man should be judged, not by what he has done, but by what one feels that he has it in him to do. Those who came under his spell were never in any doubt as to his ability. If execution sometimes fell short of conception, they were always the first to admit that the fault lay in the execution. And they were right.

In his moments of relaxation, he was the most amusing companion imaginable. He brought enormous zest and relish to everything he did. In spite of a very cutting tongue and his unconcealed personal likes and dislikes, nobody could resist him for long. In lawn-tennis circles at Queen's (he was a nearly first-class player), with the young-men-about-town, and with the racing crowd at Brooklands he was equally popular – not because of his engineering achievements, but because of something in his character which inspired liking and respect wherever he went. To those of us who knew him best, his increasing obsession with motor racing was a constant source of regret. His was a genius of too high an order to be frittered away in such a narrow field as the design of racing cars. To risk the total extinction of that genius by actually driving the things himself seemed to us nearly criminal. I do, however, believe that he got more happiness out of those last four years than many of us experience in our whole lives, so perhaps, after all, he knew what he was doing."

The rumour that Thomas was secretly married and had a daughter is rather defeated by the fact that, between the years of 1900 (when he would have been 15) and 1927, there is no marriage recorded at Somerset House in the name of John Godfrey Parry Thomas.

CHAPTER II

The Thomas Transmission

It is a little difficult, perhaps, to realise, in this era of automatic gearboxes, the very ambitious target that Thomas had set himself in 1907 when he was working on the design of his electro-mechanical transmission. Gearboxes, in general, were crude and rather unsatisfactory and, to cite a particular case, the London General Omnibus Company were not at all pleased with what they had at that time.

Thomas's solution proved eminently workable and in his youthful enthusiasm he visualised its use in vehicles of all but the smallest sizes. As has already been mentioned, he fitted it with reasonable success to the two Pipe cars and to a Delahaye, although, so far as is known, no motor manufacturer was interested enough to consider its incorporation into a standard product. Even to-day there is no reason why such a transmission should not give results that would be as good, or even better than, some of the present-day automatic transmissions. In practice, however, the production of lightweight electric motors and the delicately scaled-down switchgear required would undoubtedly be far too costly.

It seems that Thomas recognised at the time that his invention was more suited to the heavier types of transport, for a heavy lorry and later a London bus were fitted with the transmission. The most successful outcome was probably the railcar, built by

Leylands for use on the Central South African Railways and the tramcar for the Morecambe Corporation. The railcar was a handsome, if rather square-ended piece of rolling stock running on two four-wheeled bogies, while the tram was a conventional looking four-wheeled affair differing in outward appearance from its electric counterpart in the fitting of a lorry-type radiator front and rear. *The Automobile Engineer* gives the following description of the railcar:

A coach with this (Thomas) transmission has been constructed by the Leyland Company for the Central South African Railways, 37 ft. 6 in. long, and seating 42 passengers. The Leyland engine is reversible, and has six cylinders with a bore and stroke of 7 ins., developing 120 b.h.p. at 670 r.p.m., whilst it may be accelerated to give 200 b.h.p. The speed variation is effected by means of a controller, with contacts breaking in oil, operated by a hand lever in the ordinary way, and providing for starting the engine from the battery, propelling the vehicle in either direction at any speed from zero to top speed, charging the batteries whilst running at top speed, propelling the vehicle by means of dynamotor No. 2, which is supplied with current from the accumulators and applying the electrical brakes. The engine is placed midway on the vehicle and stands less than 2 ft. above the level of the frame. It is cased over and enclosed in a compartment which is reserved for the conveyance of luggage. The radiator which is built up in three sections, any one of which may be cut out of circuit if found to be faulty, is mounted upon the roof of the coach and over each section are a couple of sheet metal shields, which serve the double purpose of preventing the hot rays of the sun from bearing directly upon the radiator tubes, and inducing a current of air between the coils

16

when the vehicle is in motion. The approximate weight of the complete coach in running order is 21 tons 5 cwt.

The advantages claimed for this system are:

(1) That at no time is more than one-third of the power transmitted electrically, whilst the remainder is transmitted mechanically.

(2) There is no electrical loss on top gear.

(3) As the dynamotors transmit only a small proportion of the total power, and that only at starting and during periods of acceleration, they may be made much smaller and lighter than the motors for any other system.

(4) The engine may be stopped every time the vehicle is stopped and restarted through one of the motors for which current is supplied by the accumulators.

So far, the South African car has given great satisfaction. The coach will maintain a speed of 30 m.p.h. on a gradient of 1 in 25, whilst its acceleration with a full load on the level is 1·3 ft. per sec. Its maximum speed on the level is 50 m.p.h.

The transmission as Thomas devised it consisted of an epicyclic train coupled to a final drive with two electric motor/generators in parallel to it. The system also incorporated a dog-clutch as well as a normal one. By varying the electrical connections and thus using the units alternatively as generators or dynamos, it was possible to achieve an infinitely variable ratio.

Low ratios were given by using the first unit as a generator whereas when used as a motor it produced an overdrive. With both units isolated and the dog-clutch locked, a direct drive was achieved, and this gave a middle or normal driving ratio.

In order to achieve the various electrical combinations Thomas had thought out a most ingenious control mechanism. Beautifully

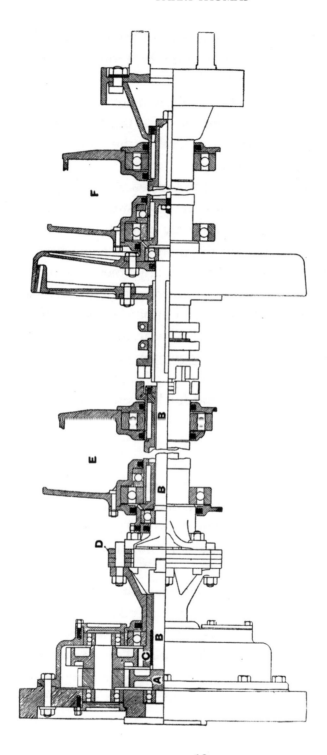

Figure 1. Diagrammatic section of the Thomas Transmission with all dynamo details omitted for the sake of clarity. A: Main Sun Wheel. B: Main Driving Shaft. C: Sleeve Sun Wheel. D: Universal Joint connecting the sleeve which carries armature of Dynamo E. F: Second Dynamo with armature on main shaft.

designed and executed, it was compact and easily serviced. It was operated by a single lever moved through a quadrant and for convenience gave a choice of ten forward speeds.

It was claimed that the efficiency over almost the whole of the range exceeded 80% rising to over 91% at the peak.

At the time *The Automobile Engineer* commented:

Needless to say, a good many advantages are claimed for this gear, particularly for lorry and omnibus work, but the drawbacks in both these cases are the cost and the weight, although neither of these are so much above that of an ordinary gearbox as might be imagined. The transmission system, however, seems to be eminently suitable for that particular class of locomotion which the internal combustion engine has hitherto been unable to exploit on account of transmission difficulties. This is, of course, light railway work. On rails, weight is a matter of very small importance, the great trouble being the need for an enormous reserve of power for starting purposes. With such a car as the Thomas it would be quite easy to start even a heavy train, and the control would not be dissimilar to that of a car with electric power. Heavy gradients could be tackled and, for light railway work in particular, the internal combustion engine has tremendous advantages over the usual steam locomotive. That this has already been realised is shown by the fact that the Leyland Co. are at present building a railway car fitted with one of their own engines and a Thomas transmission. We hope to be able to describe this machine in detail in the near future, and, in conclusion, would say that while the Thomas transmission does not appear likely to displace the gearbox for most types of motor vehicles at present in common use, it might quite possibly be found to be a means for simplifying the handling of very heavy wagons or tractors, or for railway work.

This would seem to be a very fair appraisal and the reasons given were probably the explanation of the failure of the transmission for road transport. There is little doubt that the availability of very cheap coal at that time and the lack of a suitable Diesel engine prejudiced its development for railcars.

CHAPTER III

The Leyland Eight

The idea of starting from scratch to produce a perfect motor car, with no restraint in the matter of cost, must be a designer's dream. It must also be a little difficult to decide where to begin. However, in 1917, Thomas found himself in this almost unique position and, as if that was not enough, with the services of Reid Railton as his assistant. It is not surprising therefore that a magnificent – and extremely expensive – car resulted.

Before going into details of the construction of the car itself, it will be appropriate to quote a letter which Thomas wrote to *The Autocar* in 1921 and which gives an impression of the seriousness of his intentions. He writes:

I note in the Correspondence of *The Autocar* of 4th June that a large number of car owners and others are expressing their views as to which is the world's best car. One of them asks, "Where does the Leyland Eight come in?"

As the designer of the Leyland Eight, I may say it never has been, and never will be, the makers' wish that any discussion such as this should take place, it being their intention to produce the most perfect car it is possible to design and manufacture. It may, however, interest you to know that the only car which we consider worthwhile having as a sparring partner to the Leyland Eight is the Rolls-

Royce. The Leyland Eight is not, and will not be until next year, in the hands of the public, and of the cars that are in the hands of the public, in the writer's opinion, there is not one which can hold a candle to the Rolls-Royce.

If the matter were thoroughly gone into, it would probably be found that the originator of the whole of this question has brought up the matter out of "pique". I do not, of course, know who started the correspondence.

> J.G.P. Thomas, Chief Engineer,
> Leyland Motors Ltd.

Referred to by the Press as the "Lion of Olympia", the Leyland Eight made a sensation at the 1920 Show; for, quite apart from the unusual and ingenious features in its design, it was the first eight-cylinder-in-line British touring car to be produced. The chassis alone was priced at £2500 (*8, 11*).

The engine was of 6967 c.c. with a bore and stroke of 89 by 140 mm. when the car first appeared, but was subsequently increased in size to 7266 c.c. (89 x 146 mm.), the Treasury rating being 40 h.p. (*7*). The combustion chambers were hemispherical and each contained two inclined tulip valves which were operated by an overhead camshaft. Each cam was common to one inlet and one exhaust valve. A leaf spring closed each pair of valves, the rockers being girder-like in construction and drilled for lightness. The springs themselves were not fixed in the centre but were on a rocking base, so that the opening inlet valve tended to pull the exhaust valve tighter shut, and vice versa. The cylinder head was detachable and in one piece; a three-sectioned head having been tried and discarded. The triple eccentric camshaft drive was worked by connecting rods of drilled H section. The eccentric at the top was held in a casing pivoted at one side, so that heat expansion would not affect the working of the gear. The attachment to the camshaft itself was by means of an Oldham coupling which permitted sufficient movement, and, in addition, a bolted-up coupling made possible micro-adjustment of the timing.

The crankshaft ran in six bearings, and the connecting rods were tubular and allowed lubrication under pressure to reach the gudgeon pins. With a single Zenith carburetter, the engine developed 60 b.h.p. at 1000 r.p.m. and 110 b.h.p. at 2200 r.p.m.

The scuttle carried three reservoirs, one for petrol which was fed by an Autovac from the main tank at the rear, one for gear oil which fed the gearbox by gravity, and the third was an oil tank connected with the automatic chassis lubrication system, operated by small plunger pumps actuated by the rear quarter elliptic springs. Radiator temperature was controlled by thermostat.

A single plate clutch carried the drive to a four-speed gearbox mounted on leather rings and spigoted at the rear end to limit movement. Owing to the size of the engine which it had to turn over, the starter motor was built into the gearbox. The differential was located on the end of the propeller-shaft and twin helical bevels were employed because of the splayed axleshafts. (A spiral bevel axle drive was quoted in 1921.) The rear springs were unusual in that their first action was to twist a torsion bar after which the leaves came into operation. The front springs were semi-elliptic and, like the rear ones, had no shackles, each axle being held in place by stout radius rods.

The brakes were vacuum-servo operated and could also, *in extremis*, be worked by mechanical means. The steering gear incorporated two gearboxes and allowed the shaft to run down the driver's side of the scuttle and keep itself out of the engine compartment altogether. The top box permitted any angle of rake for the steering wheel.

For the rest, Delco coil ignition was used, Smith lighting and starting, and tyres of 895 by 135 mm. were fitted to the disc wheels.

By the time it came to the Olympia Motor Show in 1921 the Leyland chassis was quoted at £1875 and the five-seater tourer at £2700.

Altogether fourteen Leyland Eight cars were made. The first one to be completed was an open four-seater with disappearing hood. The rather square-shaped radiator was relieved by rounded edges, and a great number of fine louvres made the detachable bonnet-sides look most impressive (9). The headlamp shells were given a square-ish shape to match the radiator, although the lamp glasses were round. The side lamps were similarly treated. Enormous, and rather ugly, conical hub caps were fitted and the car carried two spare wheels. This, incidentally, was the car that Thomas used in his early competitions.

Two cars were sold to the Maharajah of Patiala and, as no maintenance manuals were produced, Reid Railton had to travel to India with the cars in order to explain their working and upkeep to the Maharajah's garage staff. Michael Collins bought another which, during the trouble in Ireland, received a bullet through the windscreen, and one or two further cars were sold to wealthy purchasers in England.

Had Leylands decided to make the necessary jigs and to tool up for quantity production the price of the "Eight", which at the time must have seemed astronomical, would most certainly have been lowered considerably. This, however, was not to be, and on Stand 317 at the 1922 Motor Show the Leyland was exhibited for the last time. Two complete cars were shown: a special saloon by Vanden Plas and a five-seater coupé by Windover. The chassis price remained at £1875, and the information given in the Buyers' Guide referred to a Brolt starter, Smith carburetter, spiral final drive and a 28-gallon tank. The wheelbase was quoted as 10 ft. 6 ins., the track as 4 ft. 8 ins., and the ground clearance as 10 ins.

Other than the racing cars which Thomas constructed at Brooklands, only one other car was ever made and that was assembled by Thomson & Taylor's, after Thomas's death, from some of the remaining parts that were still available. A short-tailed body with flared wings was fitted to a racing chassis and the torsion bar mounting of the rear springs was dispensed with. The car was sold to the Hon. David Tennent.

Quite recently this machine was discovered at the back of a garage near London and was bought from its third owner, Mr. Dick Marshall, by Sir Henry Spurrier, Leyland's managing director, who handed it over to his firm's apprentices for reconditioning and "face lifting". Since the war, the car had been entered in various hill climbs and speed trials and had, in fact, been first in the unlimited sports car class at Elstree and Prescott.

The rebuilding at Leylands was superintended by Newton Iddon, a member of the research division, who, as a boy, had served four years' apprenticeship in the Leyland Eight car department. The car was in good condition mechanically, although dishevelled in appearance. Maximum wear on the cylinder bores was 0·003 in, across the diameter, although no data was available on its mileage. The crankshaft, main bearings and connecting rods were in first-class condition. The clutch required a new pressure plate but the gearbox was good. A partial strip-down of the rear axle showed that the pinion gears were perfectly bedded. According to Mr. Iddon, "despite their age, they looked like a new set of gears which had had a few weeks' running-in".

The car is now resplendent in cream paintwork with all the metal fittings chromium-plated and a high polish on its four brass carburetters. It has, at last, entered a sort of Valhalla in the form of a museum of old Leyland vehicles which is being formed by Sir Henry Spurrier[1]. It develops 200 b.h.p. at 2800 r.p.m., has a

---

[1] The car is at present on loan to the Montagu Motor Museum, Beaulieu.

compression ratio of 7 to 1 and a bore and stroke of 89 by 140 mm., giving a cubic capacity of 6920 c.c.

While Leylands are justifiably proud of this reflection of their engineering prowess in the nineteen-twenties, they could not, at the same time, have paid a more fitting tribute to the memory of Parry Thomas, nor one which would have pleased him better.

CHAPTER IV

Racing, 1922

B Y the end of 1921, with much difficulty and a great deal of persuasive argument, Thomas had jockeyed the Leyland directors into agreeing that he might enter a Leyland Eight for the Easter Monday Meeting at Brooklands the following year. They were obviously not keen on the project, but they felt that they had played safe by insisting that the car, a two-seater on the short "Speed Model" chassis, should be run in full touring trim. A demonstration of reliability and quiet running would be quite enough for the present, and its speed of around 90 m.p.h. should be sufficient to impress the spectators. They were not to know that, once having arrived at the track, their Chief Engineer would strip off every possible accessory (*12*). Half-measures were not in the Thomas tradition.

The Autocar, on 8th April, announced the prospects for the coming Easter Monday Meeting, adding that there were fewer entries than the previous Easter and continuing:

Count Zborowski and Mr. Malcolm Campbell have each entered a 4½-litre 8-cylinder-in-line Ballot; Mr. Louis Coatalen the 12-cylinder Sunbeam, 6-cylinder 4½-litre Sunbeam and one of the famous Talbot-Darracqs; and Mr. H.W. Cook, the Vauxhall "Rouge et Noir". The huge Lorraine-Dietrich and the 8-cylinder Viper are amongst other well-known cars that will be seen. Of the newcomers a straight-eight Leyland will be watched with interest.

The line up for the 28th 100-m.p.h. Short Handicap (5¾ miles) saw the Leyland and ten other cars ready to do battle for two laps. One cannot imagine that Thomas was in the least awed by the fast cars and illustrious drivers in whose company he found himself, but he would not have been human if, with a car of his own design on the starting-line for the first time, he had not felt eaten away with excitement inside. Possibly because of this, as well as a lack of experience in racing starts, the flag fell and the Leyland's clutch slipped disastrously. *The Autocar* reported the race kindly, by saying:

A field of eleven turned out for this event which, it was hoped, would give a line on the form of the Leyland "Eight" that was making its debut. Unfortunately, clutch trouble of an easily remediable nature beset it early and it did not complete the course.

RESULT:1. Kaye Don (A.C. 1496 c.c.).
2. Count Zborowski (Benz 21,501 c.c.).
3. Major H.O.D. Segrave (Sunbeam 4914 c.c.).

All the same the "easily remediable nature" of the trouble seems to have caused the Leyland to miss the next meeting on 14th May. On Saturday, 21st May, the Essex Motor Club had organised a meeting at Brooklands under the patronage of the Duke of York, and the entry lists showed that the aluminium-bodied two-seater Leyland was scheduled for three races, at 1.55 p.m., 3 p.m. and 5.25 p.m. As the Earl and Countess of Athlone were to be present (as well as the Duke of York, who was delayed by a burst tyre between London and Brooklands) the first of these races was the

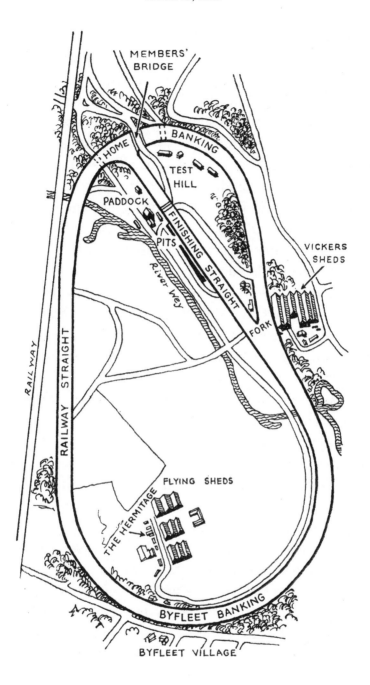

Figure 2. Diagram Brooklands Motor Course, Weybridge, Surrey.
Lap distance: 2 miles 1,350 yards.

Earl of Athlone Lightning Handicap over 8½ miles (3 laps). Thomas received 39 secs. start from the scratch man, K. Lee Guinness, with his 12-cylinder Sunbeam, and was well behind the limit car, the 10,087-c.c. Fiat driven by P. Rampon. Count Zborowski's "Chitty-Bang-Bang I" was on 21 secs. Lee Guiness burst an off-side rear tyre at speed without coming to any harm, and "Chitty-Bang-Bang's" off-side rear deflated and came off. H.W. Cook, on an 8-cylinder Ballot (5104 c.c.) came through from 30 secs. to win, followed by P. Rampon on the huge Fiat, followed by J.G.P. Thomas (Leyland), whose car, to quote a race report, "ran consistently at a fine pace but it would probably be better for a little additional stiffening of the springs". In the Duke of York Handicap (8½ miles) there is no written comment on Thomas's progress and he certainly did not finish in the first three. The Duke of York himself, owing to his personal handicap of a wheel change on the road, only arrived just as the race was finishing. However, he was able to watch the Long Handicap, named in his honour, over a course of 11 miles. Again, the Leyland was not in the money but was referred to as "travelling well but with a curious rear-wheel bounce that looked unusual". The race went to Miss Ivy Cummings (Sunbeam 3071 c.c.), who had received a start of 2 mins. 8 secs. and was well ahead of Segrave (Sunbeam 4914 c.c.) from scratch, who passed Woolf Barnato (Talbot 2614 c.c.) on the last lap as he came off the Byfleet banking.

The following Saturday, 28th May, the Essex County and Southend-on-Sea Automobile Club had organised a hill climb at Laindon, and for this Thomas had entered two cars: the two-seater he had used at Brooklands and a five-seater tourer. It would seem that a little of the Thomas ingenuity was called into play in order to comply with the regulations, as the Brooklands car was down to be driven by J.G.P. Thomas and the five-seater by a certain Mr. J.G. Parry.

The day's sport must have been confusing to the spectators as there were, in all, 23 classes, some of which were split into four or five sub-divisions, and the same cars were seen on the hill time after time. In spite of the road being long, winding, narrow and with a poor surface, the gradient was only in the neighbourhood of 1 in 8 and the fast cars came off best. Both Leyland cars, according to a contemporary journalist, "emitted an unusually fierce snarling exhaust", though this seems hardly in keeping with the normal behaviour of the 7-litre "Eight". The honours were naturally many and varied, but the names of Major Coe (Vauxhall – 32½ secs.), A. Frazer-Nash (G.N. – 29⅘ secs.), Leon Cushman (Bugatti – 32 secs.) and W. Barnato (Hispano-Suiza – 34⅗ secs.) were among the successful competitors. Thomas must have been quite satisfied with his day being second to Major Coe in Class 4 (J.G.P. Thomas – 35 secs.), second to Barnato in Class 12 (J.G. Parry – 35 secs.) and in Class 18 following Frazer-Nash and Cushman (J.G. Parry – 34 secs.). Finally, in an acceleration test consisting of a stop and restart in the middle of the hill, the result in Class 1 was:

1. Major Coe (Vauxhall)   43 secs.
2. J.G. Parry (Leyland)   45⅗ secs.
3. {L. Cushman (Bugatti)
    {J.G.P. Thomas (Leyland)   48 secs.

By the time the Whit Monday meeting at Brooklands came round, the two-seater Leyland had been fitted with two huge Hartford shock absorbers per wheel and the torsion bar assistance to the rear leaf springs had been dispensed with. The result was a distinct improvement in the track-holding qualities of the car, and at this meeting the spectators, who included in their number Prince Axel of Denmark and Lord Inverforth, were to see the Leyland win its first race at Weybridge. It also took three second places.

In view of Thomas's subsequent career at Brooklands, it is interesting to note that in the 15th Lightning Short Handicap the Leyland was the limit car with a start of 40 secs. for the two-lap race. Experienced drivers and monster engines made the handicappers hard on Count Zborowski's "Chitty-Bang-Bang" (23,092 c.c.), E.A.D. Eldridge's Isotta-Maybach (20,392 c.c.) and J.F. Duff's Fiat of 18,145 c.c. Thomas was off to a good start and looked like reaching home without being caught, but Count Zborowski thundered through the field, took the lead towards the end of the second lap and burst his off-side rear tyre. He manhandled his huge car off the banking and crossed the line a winner with rags of inner tube jammed in the brake drum and a wreath of fretted rubber round the rim. One need not elaborate on the qualities of sinew and determination that were called for in controlling these unruly and ungainly giant machines. Thomas's first and well-deserved win came in the 30th 100-m.p.h. Short Handicap (5¾ miles) when the Leyland jumped ahead of the limit car (Shipwright's S.P.A.) and maintained the lead to the end, with an average speed of 94·25 m.p.h. C.C. Brocklebank driving a Peugeot of 5803 c.c., a machine that was even then considered as a "magnificent old car", was close on his heels by the end of the race.

In the 15th Lightning Long Handicap, Thomas was both second and last. "Chitty-Bang-Bang's" wrecked wheel made it a non-starter and of the other two contenders one was eliminated in the first lap when Duff's Fiat wrecked its engine, while Eldridge in his Isotta-Maybach had an easy victory at 98·75 m.p.h. having conceded 3 secs. to the Leyland. In the last race of the day, the 29th 100-m.p.h. Long Handicap, Thomas could make no impression on Count Zborowski's 4½-litre Mercedes, which won comfortably at 97·74 m.p.h., and finished second a considerable distance astern. Quite apart from Thomas's own feelings, the

Leyland directors must have felt well satisfied with the result of the day's racing.

On Saturday, 8th July, there was a hill-climb at Holme Moss and a few excerpts from *The Autocar* of the following Friday will serve well, with one unpardonable inaccuracy, to cover the event.

From the point of view of the many spectators who, huddled under umbrellas at the vantage points – Holme Moss hill has two severe right-hand corners, besides lesser curves – the annual open event jointly run by the Bradford and Huddersfield clubs was an exciting affair. The majority of the cars entered were purely racing vehicles, or more or less standard cars "hotted up."

The event started shortly after 2 p.m., finished at 5.30 p.m. and the results on both time and formula were available before 6 p.m. The timed portion of the hill is about 1¼ miles long, the gradient approximating 1 in 6 on the first portion at the corners and about 1 in 10 on the upper reach. ...

Being confined to cars with engines of 4001 c.c. or over, Class V was naturally expected to provide some thrills. In it eight cars were running, including two 30-98 h.p. Vauxhalls, the Sunbeam racer (which has been christened the "straight-six" as it has a 6-cylinder Indianapolis engine in one of the "straight-eight" chassis built for last year's Grand Prix), H.F. Clay's 1914 Vauxhall Grand Prix racer, a 25-h.p. Talbot, and two 40-h.p. Leylands, one of which, driven by J.G.P. Thomas had a two-seater touring body and the other a four-seater. ...

Despite the streaming road, Malcolm Campbell (25-h.p. Sunbeam) managed to reduce his previous time by nearly 2 secs., and his climb in 80⅘ secs. now stands as a record for the hill. E.R. Hall (Bugatti), H. Spurrier (Leyland) and J.G.P. Thomas (Leyland) made creditable runs, whilst Harold F. Clay (Vauxhall) secured second fastest time in 91 secs.

Results	Class V	4001 c.c. & over
M. Campbell	(25-h.p. Sunbeam)	82⅖ secs.
H.F. Clay	(25-h.p. Vauxhall)	88⅗ secs.
J.G.P. Thomas	(40-h.p. Leyland)	106⅖ secs.
E.R. Hall	(25-h.p. Talbot)	(no time given)

Letter to The Autocar (21st July 1922)
Holme, Moss Hill Climb

I notice that you have described the car driven by myself as a two-seater. As a matter of fact, it was a four-seater touring car, being the original car built in 1920.

The car you referred to was the two-seater speed model which has recently been performing at Brooklands. Unfortunately, at the time of this hill-climb, that car was being fitted with a new body, and was therefore not available.

J.G.P. Thomas

The new body which had been fitted to the short chassis speed model car had for its main feature a bluntly streamlined nose behind the original square radiator while the tail tapered to a sharp point (*19*). Two leather straps secured the bonnet.

On Saturday, 22nd July, the car appeared at the Essex Motor Club's Brooklands Meeting, painted white with the chassis and wheels in light blue. The spectators were not numerous and consisted mainly of the hard-bitten habitués of the track, but the racing was good. Thomas had entered for three races, two short handicaps and one long.

The new body had its first airing in the Essex Lightning Short Handicap but the car was not running well. Kaye Don ran through the field with the Wolseley Viper (all 11,762 c.c. of it) to win, followed by H.W. Cook's Vauxhall, "Rouge et Noir". The feature of the race, from a spectacular point of view, was a gigantic Benz, one of the four racers of which L.G. Hornsted had two before World War I. It left the paddock with a carburetter fire in progress, the driver saying that it would blow out. It did, but after starting in a cloud of smoke and accelerating to a good speed, with much misfiring, it was seen to pull in to the inside of the track and burst into flames, reducing itself to a wreck. In the Essex Senior Short Handicap, the Leyland's earlier trouble developed to the point of one cylinder cutting out. After limping round for two laps, Thomas used the time before his last race to make adjustments – and extremely successful ones. For in the Essex Lightning Long Handicap his car went magnificently. At the outset the Wolseley Viper went ahead but soon threw a tyre tread. On the second lap Thomas passed on the inside and was able to hold off the determined efforts of Kaye Don, who was pressing on despite his treadless tyre. Result:

		Handicap
1.	J.G.P. Thomas (Leyland 7266 c.c.)	12 secs.
2.	Kaye Don (Wolseley Viper 11,762 c.c.)	4 secs.
3.	E.A.D. Eldridge (Fiat 10,087 c.c.)	32 secs.

With the August Meeting so near, Thomas must have had great hopes of success now that everything seemed right with the Leyland in its new guise. But the meeting was destined to be marred by the first fatal accident since the 1914-18 war and was abandoned after the eighth race. In his first race (16th Lightning Short Handicap) he had the satisfaction of securing second place, being unable to catch the Benz, driven by H.V. Barlow, which had been miraculously resuscitated after its disastrous fire during the last meeting, while in the subsequent 31st 100-m.p.h. Short Handicap something was amiss again and Thomas was forced to come in and retire. Evidently the trouble was fairly serious as the car was posted as a non-starter for the 16th Lightning Long

Handicap. Then came tragedy. A Vauxhall, with D.J. Gibson at the wheel, crashed into the fence on leaving the Byfleet banking, killing its driver and inflicting head injuries on the mechanic.

Later in the month, on Wednesday, 23rd August to be exact, there were Speed Trials at Southsea. These were organised by the Municipality as part of a charity carnival and were, in fact, the first to be run in this manner. They attracted a number of Brooklands drivers including Thomas, who throughout his life was always ready to respond to deserving charities (17). Although he unquestionably ran, details of his performance are not known. The car was back in form on 2nd September when, at the Brooklands meeting of the South East Centre of the A.C.U., it won a two-lap race at 101·02 m.p.h. from scratch, having conceded 44 secs. to the limit man, Woolf Barnato (Talbot). Later in the day the Leyland stripped its bevel gear when starting for the final of a one-lap sprint race, necessitating in all probability a visit to the Leyland works.

Four weeks elapsed before the Essex Motor Club's Championship Meeting. The object of the organisers was to discover the champion car in each class, but owing to a number of failures during practice, several potent machines were non-starters. Furthermore (quoting *The Autocar*):

> Worst of all, Count Zborowski's "Chitty-Bang-Bang" burst a front tyre in practice, became unsteerable as a result, first hit a stone parapet at the top of one part of the home banking and then charged straight down off the track, turning round as it did so. In the process the car entirely demolished the signal box at the commencement of the mile, together with the adjacent telegraph pole, losing its front axle complete in the process, and, still upright, ploughed along the grass until it came to rest some distance from the track. Zborowski was unhurt, his mechanic was thrown out and badly shaken,

while an attendant in the signal box had one hand smashed. A second attendant, with great presence of mind, lay flat, and the car jumped over him. Thus one of the fastest cars was eliminated.

In his heat (all starts being from scratch) Thomas just beat E.A.D. Eldridge's Isotta-Maybach over the two-lap course, averaging 103·75 m.p.h. But when it came to the final, in the afternoon, he was up against K. Lee Guinness with the famous 12-cylinder 18,322-c.c. Sunbeam. Nothing daunted, Thomas put up a remarkably good show, but rather naturally the Sunbeam ran away to win the Championship, clocking 104·04 m.p.h. for the 5·5 miles. Thomas was down to run in four of the handicap races later in the afternoon – two "Shorts" and two "Longs". In these races M.C. Park (Vauxhall 2996 c.c.) was the star performer, securing two firsts and two seconds. In the Essex Lightning Short, the handicappers may not have allowed for his Vauxhall being so much on top of its form for he ran away with the race, with Thomas scrapping hard but unsuccessfully with Eldridge's Isotta-Maybach and Zborowski's Ballot, which took second and third places respectively. The Leyland won the "Senior Short" from scratch at 103·18 m.p.h. passing Park's Vauxhall, which had been rehandicapped back to 8 secs. The Essex Senior Long was probably the most exciting race with Park on the 8-sec. mark, and Thomas reduced this time from scratch to "owes 8 secs." The limit car was a Hampton, driven by B.S. Marshall, who held his advantage until the final lap. Park and Thomas tore through the field, but in spite of the Leyland's greater speed Thomas was unable to do better than to obtain third place, incidentally much cheered by a delighted crowd, Park winning with another Vauxhall driven by H.W. Cook making second place from an initial advantage of 40 secs. For the last race it was Isotta, Ballot, Leyland and Vauxhall again with the addition of W.B. Horn's

Straker-Squire (3921 c.c.). Count Zborowski drove the Ballot from scratch to win easily, followed by Park and then Horn's Straker-Squire. Eldridge's huge Maybach engine cut out completely and Thomas, it appears, "suddenly slowed" which sounds ominous.

In the B.A.R.C. Final Meeting (14th October) and in perfect weather, noted at the time as being a pleasant change, the spectators had their fill of excitement. In the 17th Lightning Short, R.C. Gallop driving Count Zborowski's Ballot secured an impressive win at an impressive speed (106·5 m.p.h.). The Leyland came home second followed by the insupressible Park with his Vauxhall. Both Gallop and Park were running on an alcohol mixture. Thomas's slow getaway in the 32nd 100-m.p.h. Short Handicap spoilt his chances in spite of a fast second lap. The winning post was still in the Finishing Straight at this time and the inconvenience of this was demonstrated very pointedly in this race by J.F. Duff driving the Benz owned by J.L. Dunne. Owing to inadequate brakes he could not make the turn on to the main track after finishing and disappeared broadside over the banking, collecting a telegraph pole as he went. By great good fortune and due to the fact that the car's speed sideways was relatively slow, neither Duff nor his mechanic was very seriously hurt. The 17th Lightning Long was unusual in having only three starters, Park's Vauxhall (14 secs.), Thomas's Leyland (scratch) and Zborowski's Ballot (4 secs.). The cars finished in that order, Thomas, this time making a good start, but being unable to catch Park, whose average for the race was a very commendable 108·73 m.p.h. In the last race of the day Thomas had to give best, and also 37 secs., to both F.C. Clement's single-seater Bentley 3-litre and H.W. Cook's Vauxhall (4526 c.c.). The exertions of the day proved too much for Park's Vauxhall, which went up in alcohol-assisted flames, fortunately without hurt to the driver.

In *The Autocar's* comments on the meeting there is one remark that accentuates a difficulty always present in the nineteen-twenties but which nowadays one is apt to forget. "Tyres," they said, "are still a limiting factor, as they have been all the season, for this meeting proved that no make of cover is immune at speeds over 100 m.p.h."

There was one last race for the large cars before the track closed at the end of November. This was during the afternoon of car and motor-cycle racing organised on Armistice Day in aid of Earl Haig's Fund. It was a two-lap race run under rather dismal weather conditions. Thomas had by now improved his methods of leaving the starting line. He shot away from scratch passing, among others, Clement's Bentley and Kaye Don's Wolseley Viper, but was unable to catch Malcolm Campbell, whose Talbot (3817 c.c.) had received a start of 40 secs.

Looking back over his first season at Brooklands, Thomas must have been pleased with the result. He had been placed fourteen times, 3 firsts, 8 seconds and 3 thirds. This achievement, almost one might say without setback, proved the worth of his ability as a designer, but, as a driver in his first year of racing, starting with one of the fastest cars at the track, his record was even more impressive – no mishaps, no dangerous misjudgements, just steadily increasing success.

CHAPTER V

Racing, 1923

The new season at Brooklands saw Thomas settled in "The Hermitage". He and Kenneth Thomson, whom he had originally met during his time at the City and Guilds, had taken the bungalow inside the track from its previous owner, Capt. A.G. Miller, together with the garages attached to it (1).

Leylands had been extremely kind and understanding. They had made it quite clear that their Chief Engineer must either attend to his work at Leyland or become a racing driver at Brooklands, and Thomas had not been in two minds about his decision. The Leyland Eight was being dropped owing to the effect on finances of the trade slump and the strong feelings expressed by the shareholders as to the employment of their money. So, Thomas's contract with the firm was ended, and he was allowed to take to Weybridge several complete chassis and all the available spares and parts that he would reasonably require. The career that was to bring him so prominently into the public eye had now begun.

Much work had already gone forward and a sister car to his own Leyland was constructed for Capt. J.E.P. Howey. At the track, Thomas had met T.B. André, whose firm, with offices at 5 Dering Street, Bond Street, W.I, had taken over the construction in England of a 10-h.p. car of French origin, known as the Marlborough. Thomas had become interested in this robust little

car and co-operated with André in producing a racing version of
it (to be called the Marlborough-Thomas), by fitting it with a
larger 1982-c.c. engine which he had developed from a unit
intended for use in London taxicabs in conjunction with the
Walthamstow firm of Peter Hooker Ltd., whose managing
director was Hedley Thomson, the elder brother of his friend,
Kenneth.

The car itself was suggestive of a larger machine scaled down
(15) and had as one of its original features a chassis frame with
side members of upturned "U" section which housed the front
½-elliptic and the rear ¾-elliptic springs inside the "U", thus
eliminating the need for spring brackets. The new engine showed
a similarity to the Leyland design in having an overhead camshaft driven by twin eccentrics and valves controlled by leaf
springs. By Whitsun, two of these cars were constructed and
running.

Possibly because of all this work, Thomas's own Leyland was
not a runner at the B.A.R.C. Easter Meeting, on 2nd April.
However, Capt. Howey was able to try out his new car, driving it
in the Easter Private Competitors' Handicap and in the 33rd 100-
m.p.h. Short Handicap. Placed on the scratch mark in each case,
he was unable to gain a place, but his speed down the Railway
Straight was well over the 100-m.p.h. mark. For the Brooklands
Founders' Gold Cup (5¾ miles) Thomas took the wheel but had
no better success. It is possible that the handicappers were feeling
their way at the first meeting of the year, for the four competitors
crossed the finishing line in the order of starting – Eldridge (Fiat),
Cook (Vauxhall), Kaye Don (Wolseley Viper) and Thomas
(Leyland). In the last race of the day, Thomas tried again, but the
18th Lightning Long Handicap was not much of a race. A heavy
crop of non-starters, increased by Eldridge, who swung out from
the paddock with such verve that his Fiat burst a tyre, left only
two cars on the line. H.W. Cook's Vauxhall was an easy winner,

leaving Thomas to do his best with a Leyland that started a bout of serious misfiring.

He was able to run his own Leyland on the following Saturday as the programme of the Ealing & District M.C.C. meeting included a 3-lap "unlimited" race. The event was little more than an opportunity to draw some air through the Zenith carburetters as, with a large field of smaller cars, the Leyland in company with Le Champion's Isotta Maybach motored round with great discretion, never challenging the leaders. The race was won by C.F. Temple, driving Buchanan's Horstman, who was followed home by Capt. A.G. Miller (Wolseley). As a bit of fun, and quite possibly encouraged by his friend, Mrs. Duller, Thomas participated in the final race – an impromptu handicap for any touring car or motor cycle used and driven to the track that day. There were eleven cars in the seventeen entries and Thomas moved off in a leisurely fashion from his accustomed scratch position in a standard four-seater Leyland. Mrs. Duller, with her Amilcar, was out to win and did so by a comfortable margin, much to her satisfaction and, one may assume, to Thomas's amusement.

The appetites of enthusiasts at the B.A.R.C. Whitsun Meeting, on 21st May, must have been whetted when they realised that there were three Leyland entries. One can imagine Thomas's feelings of achievement as he watched the cars of Howey and Brocklebank get away, side by side, in the Whitsun Private Competitors' Handicap, even though neither was placed at the finish. There is considerable controversy regarding this third Leyland entry in Brocklebank's name. As there appears to have been no third racing chassis constructed, Brocklebank must either have been driving Thomas's car, which is probable, or driving a stripped tourer (and handicapped equal to Howey) which seems unlikely. With his own car, now developing 125 b.h.p. at 2200 r.p.m., he won the 5¾-mile race for the Brooklands Gold Vase at

99·5 m.p.h., threading his way neatly through a bunch of cars on the Home Banking which included Cook's Vauxhall and Le Champion's Isotta-Maybach, and sliding perceptibly as he turned from the Byfleet Banking for the final rush along the Finishing Straight. This win reduced his handicap in the 19th Lightning Short from 15 secs. to 5 secs. and this, combined with rather a slow start, prevented him from getting among the leaders. The race had its compensation, however, as it was won by Howey's Leyland at 98·25 m.p.h.

In a previous race (the 23rd 75-m.p.h. Short Handicap) one of the Marlborough-Thomas cars had run. Placed on scratch and driven by T.B. André, the car proved recalcitrant and was beset by ignition trouble.

The 33rd 100-m.p.h. Long Handicap provided Thomas with a novel experience; that of starting (rehandicapped to "owes 13 secs.") on level terms with another Leyland (Capt. Howey's). He took his car very high on the banking in an attempt to beat the handicappers, but in spite of his efforts the race went to Capt. G.E.T. Eyston (Aston Martin, 1488 c.c.) at 92·25 m.p.h., second and third places being filled by Cook's Vauxhall and Clement's Bentley.

In the 19th Lightning Long Handicap, four of the largest cars were challenged by Cook's Vauxhall. A. Ellison's Lorraine-Dietrich was the first car away (40 secs.) then Cook, then Le Champion's Isotta-Fraschini and Barclay's Ballot. Thomas was last away with the Leyland and, having passed the Ballot, remained in fourth place while the order in front of him changed several times until the cars passed the post – Isotta-Fraschini, Vauxhall, Lorraine-Dietrich.

The hill climb up Two Church Hill, Laindon, organised by the Essex County and Southend A.C., was scheduled for 26th May, and for this Thomas had entered the Brooklands Leyland; (no "Mr. J.G. Parry" this year!). The spectators at this rather cumbrous

43

meeting with its multiple classes and subclasses must have worried the officials considerably by their foolhardy desire to stand in the road. They had wandered at will during the runs of the Bugattis of Densham and Mays, and only by much shouting and pushing was enough room made for the big Leyland which ascended, showering stones as its driver accelerated. There being no banner across the road at the finish, Thomas passed the timekeepers' box without noticing it and roared on to where the road terminated in a "T" junction, the right-hand arm of which formed the loop road back to the start. Instantaneously choosing the easier turn to the left, Thomas brought his car to a standstill after hitting two motor cycles and damaging the heel of a policeman's boot. The constable's opinion that several people were lucky still to be there presumably included himself in the number. The results for Class N were:

1. J.G.P. Thomas (Leyland 39·2 h.p.)   32 secs.
2. Raymond Mays (Bugatti 11·9 h.p.)   34 secs.

The meeting at Brooklands on 2nd June, held by the Essex Motor Club, was notable for the cold, dull weather, the paucity of spectators and for magnificent driving on Thomas's part. Having entered for four events, he won three of them, putting in a lap during his final race at 117 m.p.h.

His first success was in the Easter Senior 100-m.p.h. Short Handicap. Tommy Hann (Lanchester) was first away and established what looked like an unbeatable lead. Among the nine competitors was a woman driver, Mrs. O.S. Menzies, driving a large Peugeot and apparently driving it well. Eldridge's Fiat, which had overcome a bout of misfiring, surged to the fore but was overtaken by Thomas on his way to catch Hann who, at the last moment, had to be content with second place. Thomas's winning speed was 100·5 m.p.h. As a result, the Leyland was rehandicapped by a further 3 secs. for the Essex Lightning Short, but this did not prevent it crossing the line first (at 101·5 m.p.h.) in front of Cook's Vauxhall. In his third race (Essex Senior 100-m.p.h. Long Handicap) Thomas was put back from scratch to minus 15 secs. and this flattering penalty of success tipped the scales against him. He drove, according to report, "at a tremendous pace" but to no avail. Four cars lined up for the final race of the meeting, the Essex Lightning Long Handicap. The Aston Martin of Capt. Eyston took the lead followed by Cook's Vauxhall and the Leyland, both of which had passed Malcolm Campbell's Ballot. Once again Thomas finished in first place; this time his average for the race was much higher – 107·75 m.p.h. A small item of passing interest in the day's programme was that the Marlborough-Thomas (driver C.B. Brocklebank) was marked as a non-starter.

The Leyland was still on the top of its form when it came to the B.A.R.C. Summer Meeting on 23rd June. After participating, but to no special effect, in the 35th 100-m.p.h. Short Handicap, in which J.D. Barclay thrilled the crowd by an ill-judged but spectacular turn from the Byfleet Banking into the finishing straight to gain second place behind Clement's Bentley, Thomas made a mark in Brooklands history in the subsequent 20th Lightning Long Handicap. In this event varying sorts of trouble had overtaken all the competitors except the two Leylands of Howey and Thomas. Howey was in front and going well but Thomas was preparing to do even better. With his foot hard down and without a tread on either of his rear tyres, he flashed by the post a winner, and not only that but the winner of the fastest race ever won, up to then, at Brooklands, his average being 115·25 m.p.h.

On the following Saturday (30th July) he was competing at the Surbiton Motor Club's Meeting at the track with continued success, and providing what the Press, in rather blasé fashion, referred to as "his usual thrills". He could manage no better than fifth place in the Surrey Lightning Handicap, but he remedied this by a win at 110·43 m.p.h. in the Surrey Senior Lightning Long Handicap which, owing to several non-starters, turned out to be a duel between the Leyland and W. Fiennes' Bentley, the latter having a start of 68 secs. Only four cars drove out to the start for the Surrey Junior Lightning Long Handicap. They were du Heaume's Moth I, Capt. A.G. Miller's Wolseley I, T. Hann's Lanchester and Howey's Leyland driven by Thomas, who had no difficulty in winning at a speed of 108·03 m.p.h.

The Leyland was now being put to work in earnest, for Thomas had already started using the car for record breaking. One might almost believe that the radiator water never got cold, for on the following Saturday (7th July) Thomas was trying his hand at the hill climb up Spread Eagle Hill organised by the Hampshire Automobile Club. The F.T.D. went to H.W. Cook's T.T. Vauxhall, "Rouge et Noir", which managed a time of 43 secs. Malcolm Campbell, whose 6-cylinder Sunbeam had broken the record the previous year with 41⅖ secs., was slower this time, owing to two cylinders momentarily cutting out at the start, and registered 44⅕ secs. Capt. A. Frazer-Nash driving "Kim" (fitted with the engine from his "Mowgli") put up 44 secs. which beat Thomas's time by ⅘ sec., the Leyland being slow on the initial get-away.

Among the entries for the B.A.R.C. August Meeting, on 6th August, was a huge 27-litre monster that was in the future to mean so much to Thomas (30). This was the Liberty-engined Higham Special which had been built at Count Zborowski's country residence; Clive Gallop being responsible for the frame and general layout of the machine. The car had pleasing, if titanic, proportions and was intended not so much for track racing as for straight sprints like those at Fanoe Island. The gearbox came from Zborowski's huge Benz and the method of starting the engine, a considerable problem in itself, was two-fold. There was a small starting handle just aft of the near-side front wheel which turned the motor over slowly through reduction gearing or, alternatively, there was a starter motor operated from the batteries of a service lorry. Preliminary trials had shown that there was too much whip in the frame and that the radiator cowl over-restricted the passage of air for cooling purposes. Owing to the Count being abroad until shortly before the Bank Holiday, the car could not be prepared in time and was therefore a non-starter.

Thomas's first drive was at the wheel of a Marlborough-Thomas in the first heat of the 25th 75-m.p.h. Long Handicap. Situated somewhere in the middle of the race, he entered the Finishing Straight amongst a bunch of other competitors and narrowly missed a collision with B.S. Marshall's Bugatti.

Only three cars started in the 21st Lightning Short Handicap. Le Champion with his red 20,392-c.c. Isotta-Fraschini made the most of his 16 secs. start and roared away round the track for six whole seconds before the next car, Capt. J.E.P. Howey's Leyland, left the line. Later still, Thomas (on 3 secs.) joined in the fray. By the end of the first lap Le Champion was still well in front, but in the course of the second round Thomas was seriously cutting down his lead, making his final bid as he swooped down from the banking and chased the Isotta down the straight. Le Champion was just able to get home by 40 yards.

In the 35th 100-m.p.h. Long Handicap, Thomas was again second. The limit man, Major L. Ropner in his elegant all-aluminium bodied 30/98 Vauxhall, "Silver Arrow", held the lead from start to finish while Thomas, who started as favourite from his accustomed scratch position, worked his way steadily and at great speed through the field. A win for the Leyland seemed to the onlookers just possible until the last few seconds proved that it could not be done. The others streamed over the line behind him: Clement (Bentley), Perkins (Sunbeam), Le Champion (Isotta-Fraschini), Hawkes (Lorraine-Dietrich), Howey (Leyland), Rampon (Fiat), and Brocklebank (Peugeot).

The Leyland was entered for two more races but, first, in the Final of the 25th 75-m.p.h. Long Handicap (for the President's Gold Plate), its offside rear tyre deflated on the line, compelling Thomas to return to the paddock; and then, in the 21st Lightning Long Handicap, the worst happened. After one lap of competition with the Isotta-Fraschini's 20,392 c.c., Howey's Leyland's 7266 c.c. and Brocklebank's Peugeot's 5655 c.c., the crankshaft broke and the racing and the Leyland were both finished for the day.

At the beginning of September, Thomas crossed to Boulogne for the Automobile Week there which opened with three short-distance events for all classes. In the morning there was a run of 3 kilometres (flying start) over a road with switchback tendencies, followed by 1 kilometre on the level (standing start) and, in the afternoon, a 500-metres hill climb (standing start) in the town itself, up a street with houses on both sides. An aggregate time was taken for the three runs, and the Leyland clocked the fastest time of the day with 2 mins. 3 secs., averaging 110 m.p.h. for the 3-kilometre event, only to be disqualified. The runner-up, Rigal on a Panhard Levassor, in the 5000-c.c. class protested on the grounds that Thomas had changed his wheels after the first run. The rule was quite clear and the judges had no option but to disqualify the Leyland. Thomas had, in fact, overlooked this point and, not being warned by the marshals, had fitted smaller wheels mainly to save the other set for further work at Brooklands, replacements being difficult to obtain. *The Autocar* reporter loyally suggested that the change put him at a disadvantage, but in view of the shortness of the later runs it would seem that Rigal's protest was quite justified. It looks very much as if, for once in his life, Thomas was trying to be too clever. The seriousness of the tyre problem is emphasised by the fact that in the Spanish Grand Prix that year Dubonnet, the winner, changed seven tyres. Gamier burst eight and Boyriven, on a third Hispano-Suiza made fourteen changes.

The results, which show that the affair attracted a large number of competitors from England, are interesting as a comparison of contemporary machines. They were as follows:

Short Distance Tests

1.	Thomas (Leyland over 5000 c.c.)	2 mins. 03 sec. disqualified
2.	Rigal (Panhard Levassor 5000 c.c.)	2 mins. 05 sec.
3.	Clement (Bentley 3000 c.c.)	2 mins. 12⅘ secs.
4.	Du Fourmentin (La Perle 1500 c.c.)	2 mins. 13⅘ secs.
5.	Segrave (Sunbeam 2000 c.c.)	2 mins. 14⅖ secs.
6.	{Rigal (Panhard Levassor 3000 c.c.)	{2 mins. 16⅘ secs.
	{Summers (Vauxhall 4900 c.c.)	{2 mins. 16⅘ secs.
7.	Camous (Ford 3000 c.c.)	2 mins. 18 secs.
8.	Eyston (Aston Martin 1500 c.c.)	2 mins. 21 secs.
9.	Benoist (Salmson 1100 c.c.)	2 mins. 22 secs.
10.	Coe (Vauxhall 4900 c.c.)	2 mins. 24 secs.
11.	Masurel (Bugatti 1500 c.c.)	2 mins. 28⅕ secs.
12.	{Marshall (Bugatti 1500 c.c.)	{2 mins. 30 sec.
	{Dore (Senechal 1100 c.c.)	{2 mins. 30 sec.
13.	Vernier (Salmson 1100 c.c.)	2 mins. 31⅖ sec.
14.	Senechal (Senechal 750 c.c.)	2 mins. 31⅘ sec.
15.	Pagniez (Janvier over 5000 c.c.)	2 mins. 35⅕ sec.
16.	Martin (Bignan 2000 c.c.)	2 mins. 36⅖ sec.
17.	Morgan (Aston Martin 1500 c.c.)	2 mins. 36⅗ sec.
18.	Lucas (Frazer-Nash 1100 c.c.)	2 mins. 38 sec.
19.	Frazer-Nash (Frazer-Nash 1100 c.c.)	2 mins. 39 sec.
20.	Marie (Bugatti 1500 c.c.)	2 mins. 44⅘ sec.
21.	Hodgson (Hodgson 1500 c.c.)	2 mins. 45⅗ sec.

22. Senechal (Senechal 750 c.c.)   2 mins. 46⅕ sec.
23. Callard (Chenard-Walcker
         under 3500 c.c.)   2 mins. 50⅖ sec.
24. Paris (Chenard-Walcker
         under 3500 c.c.)   2 mins. 53⅖ sec.
25. {Duray (D'Aoust 1100 c.c.)   {2 mins. 53⅘ sec.
     {Eaton (Frazer-Nash 1100 c.c.)   {2 mins. 53⅘ sec.

*   *   *

The date of the last B.A.R.C. meeting of the year was altered to Wednesday, 26th September, and as a consequence the attendance was poor. The racing, however, was well up to standard although Thomas treated his first event (37th 100-m.p.h. Short Handicap) rather lightly by carrying a cinema operator with him. He followed behind Howey's sister car which managed a creditable second place behind G.A. Vandervell's four-seater Talbot. Whether Howey's lurid slide down the banking almost on top of Cook's Vauxhall was recorded on film would be difficult to discover after the lapse of so many years. In the 22nd Lightning Short Handicap Thomas gave away 9 secs. to Howey, who must have driven with great determination, crossing the line first with the complete tread of his near-side front tyre coiled round his front axle, averaging 102·25 m.p.h. Thomas himself made a fast run but could not catch H.W. Cook's Vauxhall, which had started with a credit of 19 secs. and came in second. It was definitely Howey's day for he scored another win in the 36th 100-m.p.h. Long Handicap, starting a mere 3 secs. ahead of Thomas, who was unplaced. The 22nd Lightning Long Handicap was interesting in that Howey very sportingly lent his Leyland to Count Zborowski for the event. This resulted in quite a tussle between Zborowski and Thomas, settled in Thomas's favour, the latter being able to nip past Brocklebank's Peugeot as the cars entered the Finishing Straight and take second place to Ellison's Lorraine-Dietrich, which had a runaway win from the 37-sec. mark.

In the Essex Motor Club's meeting on the following Saturday it was most unusual to see Thomas posted as a non-starter in the Essex Lightning Short Handicap. The Leyland was obviously out of action for that day, as in the Essex Lightning Long Handicap Howey handed his own car over to Thomas. The race was reported at the time to be "one of the most thrilling ever watched at Brooklands", and from the start Thomas set about shortening the initial 21-sec. lead of the Miller driven by Count Zborowski. Up to the end of the second lap the Peugeot of Mrs. Menzies was out in front, followed by a pack of cars which included Clement's Bentley, Perkins' Sunbeam, Cook's Vauxhall and Malcolm Campbell's Ballot. As the third lap began, the Miller was closing on the field and the Leyland was closing on the Miller. Passing car after car and running high on the Byfleet Banking, Zborowski still led Thomas, who was baulked by slower cars. However, as he came off the Banking on to a clear track, Zborowski pulled over to let the Leyland by to win at 109 m.p.h. Eight cars led by the Miller crossed the line in mass formation.

The only event left to be run now was the 200-Miles Race which was scheduled for Saturday, 13th October. Thomas and Duller were driving Marlborough-Thomas cars which attracted a certain amount of attention from the press owing to their Leyland-style Hooker-Thomas engines, their torsion-bar front springing and the fact that Thomas had installed a planetary gear between clutch and gearbox giving a 15% reduction to enable speed to be maintained on the rise leading to the Members' Banking. The cars were beautifully streamlined and had staggered seats, a fairing behind the driver's head and a full-length underpan. Thomas had designed a special crankshaft to bring the 1982-c.c. engines down to the 1½-litre limit, but unfortunately these items were not ready until the last moment, the chassis having to be run in with the larger engines.

Hasty preparation at the eleventh hour made success unlikely, and the race had not long started before both Duller and Thomas were struggling with sick motor cars. Ignition trouble beset both of them, Thomas making two stops in an attempt to cure misfiring while Duller drove doggedly on, on three cylinders, only to retire after 60 laps. Thomas dropped out with 45 laps completed. The race, excellently described in W. Boddy's book, *The 200-Mile Race*, was won that year by C.M. Harvey on an Alvis at 93·29 m.p.h.

Looking back over the year's sport, Thomas had come a long way in both experience and success since his previous season. He was now a well-known and well-liked personality at the track and his successes had sown seeds in the public enclosure that were so soon to blossom out into unrestrained hero-worship.

At the end of the year came the Motor Show at Olympia. There was, of course, no Leyland exhibited, but Thomas would certainly have been seen on Stand 69 where the Marlborough and Marlborough-Thomas cars were displayed (*14*). *The Autocar* gave the following details:

STAND 69
MARLBOROUGH & MARLBOROUGH-THOMAS
Country of origin – France.
T.B. André & Co. Ltd., 5 Bering Street, W.1.
Specification. 9·5 h.p., 4 cyl., 62 by 91 mm. (1099 c.c.), tax £10, forced lubrication, plate clutch, Bosch magneto ignition, Cozette carburetter, 3 speeds, separate gearbox, spiral-bevel back-axle drive, ½-elliptic front and ¼-elliptic rear springs, 700 by 80 mm. tyres on disc wheels, Bleriot electric lighting and starting. Price: Chassis £160. Standard two-seater £175.
Features. Extremes meet here, for there is on the one hand the

Marlborough chassis which, with electric lighting and starting and four shock absorbers, is priced at only £160, and on the other the Marlborough-Thomas racing car having a chassis price of £575, though the engine of the second is but 50% greater in size than the first. The second car is, however, capable of exceedingly high speeds. The Marlborough is a cleanly designed job, light and strong.

Specification. 12·1 h.p., 4 cyl., 70 by 97 mm. (1493 c.c.), tax £13, forced lubrication, disc clutch, C.A.V. coil ignition, spiral-bevel back-axle drive, torsional front and rear springs, 32 by 4 in. tyres on wire wheels, Blériot electric lighting and starting. Price: Chassis: £575. Standard two-seater £675.

Features. As an example of streamlining the Marlborough-Thomas sports car, which is identical with the 200-miles racer save for the fitting of flared wings, would be hard to beat. For road work small windscreens and a hood are added. The car possesses several special features, notably the Hooker-Thomas engine, which has included overhead valves operated through a twin eccentric-driven overhead camshaft. The springing is unusual, being a method of attaching the axles to the frame through arms attached to the ends of the transverse members which spring torsionally. A useful feature of this suspension is that the ground clearance of the car can be altered from a very low position to a relatively normal one by a few hours' work on adjustments.

CHAPTER VI

Racing, 1924

Thomas's workshops must have been extremely busy during the winter months. The main job had been the almost complete redesigning of the Leyland. The car was now to appear as the Leyland-Thomas No. 1, with a much lower body, for which a saving in head resistance of 40% was claimed, and a long pointed tail (21). In this guise it was to become famous as the most successful car that the track had ever seen; one might almost say, was ever to see. Behind the oval opening of the streamlined cowl nestled a new circular radiator, while under the bonnet the straight-eight engine had undergone considerable modification. A redesigned crankshaft permitted the raising of the compression ratio to 7·5 to 1 and dealt with the 200 b.h.p. now obtainable at 2800 r.p.m. To produce this power four Zenith carburetters were fitted while the exhaust and inlet ports and the camshaft were redesigned. The car was painted white with the chassis, underparts and the six-stud flat-disc wheels in blue.

A Thomas Special had also been produced, having been originally designed for the 1923 200-Miles Race, using the 1½-litre Hooker-Thomas engine. Its body bore a strong resemblance to the new Leyland-Thomas, including the oval-mouthed front cowling and was painted in the same blue and white colours. The wheels were of the same flat-disc type, secured by four bolts. The short wheelbase together with the narrowness of the body gave a rather hump-backed appearance to the car (16). Using an M.A.B. chassis, Thomas had evolved a system of torsion-bar springing. He had retained the epicyclic gear train in conjunction with the normal gearbox from the previous Marlborough-Thomas. The 4-cylinder 1493-c.c. engine had a bore and stroke of 70 by 97 mm., eight overhead valves, a Zenith carburetter, Bosch ignition, K.L.G. plugs and Houdaille shock absorbers.

Thomas's first public appearance this year was at the hill climb at Kop on 29th March in a biting north-east wind. The Thomas Special, it seems, made a reasonably good climb and quite a lot of blue smoke. In the large car class, in which Count Zborowski's Ballot was a runner, Thomas drove a Leyland, but to judge from a very perfunctory reference to the car by the press it was presumably not the Leyland-Thomas. The fastest time of the day went to H.W. Cook's Vauxhall.

An innovation at the B.A.R.C. Easter Meeting, at the request of the drivers, was the elimination of the final run down the Finishing Straight in the fastest races. These races now terminated at the Vickers shed; a safety precaution appreciated by competitors if not by the spectators.

The Leyland-Thomas, due to an error on the entry form, did not run, and Thomas contented himself with the handling of the Thomas Special and Rapson's angular, 6178-c.c. Lanchester which had been evolved mainly for testing Rapson tyres and had the appearance of a cross between a racing monster and an armoured vehicle (27). The Easter Private Competitors' Handicap, won by Count Zborowski in a Bugatti, had two Leylands running in it, J.E.P. Howey's car and another entered in the name of his brother, R.B. Howey. The 38th 100-m.p.h. Short Handicap was interesting for several reasons. In it, Dario Resta made his reappearance at the track at the wheel of a straight-eight Sunbeam, J.E.P. Howey drove Thomas's Thomas Special, going well until the car started to misfire, and Thomas himself managed to take second place in the Lanchester behind Major Coe's Vauxhall. The scratch man was Count Zborowski with his Higham Special whose race finished halfway down the Railway Straight on the first lap when his near-side rear tyre left the wheel and followed the car for quite a distance. This did not deter him from securing third place in the subsequent 23rd Lightning Short Handicap (the race for the Brooklands Founders' Gold Cup) with four tyres and all the 27,059 c.c.

Thomas drove the Lanchester to victory at 92·25 m.p.h. in the 13th 90-m.p.h. Short Handicap thanks to Count Zborowski, who, having overtaken the entire field in his 2-litre Bugatti, failed to turn into the Finishing Straight, thinking that it was a "long" race instead of a "short". In the 37th 100-m.p.h. Long Handicap, Thomas was at the wheel of his Thomas Special, which seemed to run reasonably well but finished amongst the field. This car was out again on 3rd May for the J.C.C. Meeting. First of all, driven by Mrs. Duller in the Ladies' Race (sadly depleted to three runners for one reason and another) it toured round with a badly slipping clutch, then, after a little attention, Thomas brought it in third in the Junior Long Handicap. When the stewards had complained that the exhaust was too noisy, Thomas quickly satisfied them by hammering up the end of the pipe to a certain extent.

It was most unusual for Thomas not to attend a meeting for which he had sent in entry forms but, for reasons that will probably never now be known, both the Leyland and the Thomas Special were non-starters at the Aston Hill Climb on 17th May organised by the Herts County A.C. At the following week-end, the Ealing and District M.C.C. provided two car races in their day's sport at Brooklands, and the Leyland-Thomas was there on the scratch mark for the 3-lap race. The competing cars were fairly well assorted. There was the 12-litre Wolseley Viper driven by G.N. Norris, Duller's Bugatti, an Alvis driven by C.M. Harvey, Miller's Bianchi and an Ansaldo with full touring equipment and Rex Mundy at the wheel. R.W. Spiers (Morris Cowley) was first away with a stupendous handicap of 3 mins. 5 secs. which enabled him to lap Thomas before the Leyland was flagged away. This, however, did not prevent Thomas from coming in third behind the Alvis and the Bugatti.

The Whit Monday Meeting at Brooklands (9th June) was most unfortunately marred by a fatal accident when J.H. Toop, driving C.G. Brocklebank's Peugeot, went over the top of the Byfleet Banking during the 38th 100-m.p.h. Long Handicap. The meeting was thereupon abandoned.

In two of the early races, the Whitsun Light Car Handicap (5¾ miles) and the 14th 90-m.p.h. Short Handicap, George Duller driving a second Thomas Special, differing from the other only in having an uncowled radiator of Bugatti-ish shape, secured second place in each. In the second event it is interesting to note that the Thomas Special started on level terms with Blackstock's 1496-c.c. Bugatti which it was unable to hold, and with Capt. A.G. Miller's 1996-c.c. Bianchi which it managed to beat. The Leyland-Thomas had one run (in the 24th Lightning Short Handicap), but had to give best to Brocklebank's ill-fated Peugeot (5832 c.c.), Eldridge's Fiat (21,714 c.c.) and Howey's Leyland. Then ten cars left the Railway Start for the 38th 100-m.p.h. Long Handicap, Thomas driving the Lanchester with a handicap of 27 secs. The race seemed fated before the start, when Clive Gallop's Ballot caught fire momentarily, although this did not prevent his competing – or, in fact, winning the race. Ellison (Lorraine-Dietrich) and Thomas tussled strenuously during the first lap while the Ballot overtook Benjafield's Bentley. The crowd was alarmed by the Lanchester doing a lurid skid as it disappeared behind the Members' Hill amongst a batch of other cars. Thomas, however, had the situation under control, and all the cars appeared under the Members' Bridge running in an orderly fashion. Then, on the last lap, with two or three cars still to overhaul, Gallop's Ballot slowed slightly as he waited an opportunity to pass. At this moment, Toop's Peugeot, following in the Ballot's wake, was seen to hurtle over the banking and burst into flames. Gallop won the race without being aware of the tragedy, but Thomas must have been heavy-hearted as he crossed the line in second place. In the paddock, he was accosted by what can only be described as "a fool of a woman" whose great worry was whether her bet would be paid in spite of the accident. Showing considerable self-control, Thomas made some non-committal reply and used his standard tactics for dealing with people for whom he had no use, by merely walking away.

Later on, in June there were two days of speed trials on the beach at Skegness. The second day's events concerned the large cars and the heats were run off with three cars at a time. In Class II, the contestants included Malcolm Campbell's 12-cylinder Sunbeam, now fitted with a long streamline tail, Howey's Leyland, Cook's Vauxhall and the Leyland-Thomas. Miss Ivy Cummings, driving a Frazer-Nash, put up an extraordinarily good performance, actually beating Howey's Leyland by virtue of the Nash's rapid acceleration. The result of this heat was the strange spectacle of Miss Cummings lining up with Campbell's and Thomas's giants in the final stage of the competition. The result was a foregone conclusion. Campbell won easily with the 18,322-c.c. Sunbeam, creating a record for the course, and Thomas was an easy second.

At the end of the same week, on Saturday, 21st June, there were further speed trials on the sands between Saltburn and Marshe, run by the Yorkshire Automobile Club. The results in Class M (flying start) for unlimited racing cars were as follows:

1. M. Campbell   15⅖ secs. = 145·26 m.p.h.
   (Sunbeam 18,322 c.c.)
2. E.A.D. Eldridge   16 secs. = 139·81 m.p.h.
   (Fiat 21,714 c.c.)
3. J.G.P. Thomas   17⅘ secs. = 125·67 m.p.h.
   (Leyland-Thomas 7266 c.c.)

At the end of his run, Thomas received a most unpleasant cut in the face when the timing thread mounted the streamline nose of his car instead of breaking on contact as it should have done. It was most likely to have been because of this injury that the Leyland-Thomas did not make its scheduled appearance at the Hampshire A.C.'s Open Hill Climb on Spread Eagle Hill on Saturday, 28th June.

Henley clashed with the B.A.R.C. Midsummer Meeting (5th July) and the attendance at the track was consequently somewhat reduced. The new silencer regulations were now being strenuously enforced and the starts were varied, some being at the pond and some on the Railway Straight. Thomas's track tactics had by now reached the state of perfection and with the Leyland-Thomas running well there was almost no holding him. (A forward facing tube now protruded through the radiator cowl to give a form of forced induction. Though seemingly successful from the day's results, Thomas subsequently removed it.)

His first run at this meeting was in the 25th Lightning Short Handicap in which he conceded 10 sees, to Clive Gallop (Ballot) and 12 seconds to Count Zborowski (Mercedes). The Isotta-Maybach, the only other runner, petered out after the start, leaving the Mercedes out in front, hotly pursued by the Ballot. Thomas bided his time in the rear until the moment came to hustle past both cars and score a decisive win at 109·25 m.p.h. He might have repeated the performance in the 39th 100-m.p.h. Long Handicap had it been a trifle longer, for his calculations were upset by having to brake hard to avoid a bunch of slower cars forming a small traffic block far too high on the Banking. The race went instead to Malcolm Campbell's Ballot. The Leyland-Thomas had an unobstructed run in the 25th Lightning Long Handicap, starting from "owes 8 seconds", when his antagonists were once again Zborowski's 14,778-c.c. Mercedes and Gallop's 4817-c.c. Ballot. The Mercedes, getting away 30 secs. before Thomas, led the way for the first two laps until its silencer burst when the Count slowed momentarily, thinking he had seen flying pieces of tread out of the corner of his eye, but immediately pressed on again. In his final swoop on to the Railway Straight, Thomas was past both cars and won at an average of 117 m.p.h. To add to his success, he had broken the lap record at 125·14 m.p.h.

Six open events for cars were included in the South East Centre, A.C.U. Meeting organised by the Surbiton M.C. on 19th July and, of course, Thomas was there. The Leyland-Thomas worked its way through a field rather depleted by non-starters, in the Surrey Lightning Short Handicap, to win from Duller's Bugatti and Miller's Bianchi at 115·03 m.p.h. That Thomas had to travel fast to accomplish his win is shown by his fastest lap, which was at a speed of 124·8 m.p.h. Duller had previously scored a third place with his Thomas Special, and in the first of the 3-lap events Thomas himself drove the car but did not seem able to do much with it. In the next race, he drove the Rapson Lanchester from scratch, giving R.E.O. Hall's Austin Seven 1 min. 15 secs. start. The field this time consisted mostly of smaller cars including R.C. Morgan's Aston Martin and Norman Black's G.N. For two laps Thomas pursued and then, on the third lap, he took the Lanchester through the entire field to win at 98·23 m.p.h., the Austin Seven being second. In the last race the Leyland-Thomas was the only starter out of the original six entries and the race was made up by late entries – Duller (Bugatti), Morgan (Aston Martin), Hann (H.P.) and Norris (Bianchi). The race went to the

Bugatti, Thomas being unable to make an impression on the handicaps meted out to his opponents.

Owing to heavy bookings of the track, the Essex Motor Club held their annual Brooklands meeting on Wednesday, 23rd July, and provided five events for cars. In the Essex Senior Short Handicap, the Leyland-Thomas gave away as much as 1 min. 30 secs. to Ashcroft's Darracq and, starting last as usual, Thomas had to put in a lap at 125·45 m.p.h. to get into position for his final swoop from the Home Banking which brought him first past the post in the Railway Straight at an average speed of 115·15 m.p.h. The win put him to "owes 2 secs." in the Essex Senior Long Handicap and, before starting, he was lapped by Ashcroft's Darracq which had been running for most of its 2 mins. 29 secs. start. The Salmson of O. Wilson-Jones ran extremely well, and with its handicap of 1 min. 50 secs. proved uncatchable. Thomas tried very hard, breaking the lap record again on his second round at 125·77 m.p.h. and coming in second. The Essex 30-Miles Handicap (11 laps) made a pleasant change from routine, and for this Thomas brought his Thomas Special to the line with a credit of 1 min. 14 secs. The other cars were mostly of the same size, there being two Horstmans, a small Bianchi, a Clyno, an Alvis, a Wolseley and Gordon England's Austin Seven. The handicappers did a good job and the race was closely contested, Thomas pulling ahead of Purdy's Horstman to win at 82·04 m.p.h.

Rather doubtful weather on 4th August did nothing to spoil exciting racing during the B.A.R.C. August Bank Holiday Meeting. In the August Private Competitors' Handicap, George Duller won easily in his Thomas Special at 85·75 m.p.h. beating F. Scriven (Austin Twenty) and J. Benjafield (Bentley). So Thomas, although he could do no good with the Lanchester in the 41st 100-m.p.h. Short Handicap, must have started the day feeling quite pleased. Driving the Leyland-Thomas in the 26th Lightning Short Handicap, he had Campbell's Sunbeam (to which he gave 23 seconds) and Ropner's Vauxhall to contend with. In the course of tearing after the Sunbeam, which he failed to catch by 20 yards, he broke the lap record with a speed of 127·38 m.p.h. In the next race (40th 100-m.p.h. Long Handicap) he broke it again, in the unsuccessful pursuit of G.A. Vandervell's Talbot, at no less a speed than 128·36 m.p.h. In both these races the Leyland's second placings were due to inadvertent baulking by bunches of slower cars. He was out again in the 16th 90-m.p.h. Long Handicap with the Lanchester, and, although he managed to run through most of the field, passing, amongst others, Duller in his Thomas Special, he could only manage third place. The result being:

		Handicap
1.	V. Gillow (Riley)	1 min. 0 sec.
2.	K. Don (A.C.)	34 secs.
3.	J.G.P. Thomas (Lanchester)	Scratch
	Winner's speed: 81·5 m.p.h.	

He drove his own Thomas Special in the race for the President's Gold Plate (30th 75-m.p.h. Long Handicap) but finished among the also-rans. The Leyland-Thomas started in the last race of the day (26th Lightning Long Handicap) but, as the engine kept cutting out, Thomas was forced to come in and retire. After prolonged running, which included a good deal of record work, the effort of breaking the lap record twice in one afternoon had proved a little more than even a 7-litre Leyland could manage.

At the very end of August came the Boulogne Automobile Week, an event for which Thomas always had a soft spot in spite of the accident to himself and the tragedy to his friend R.B. Howey that were to come in the future, and the spot of bother over his disqualification the previous year. This, however, was the one occasion when everything went right. In the short distance speed tests, comprising 3 kilometres of undulating and indifferent road, 1 kilometre on the level and 500 metres of hill climb (all from a standing start) the Leyland-Thomas came out on top. Thomas's aggregate time for the three events was 1 min. 43⅕ sec. which meant covering the 3 kilometres at 127·57 m.p.h., the kilometre at 76·08 m.p.h. and ascending the 500 metres in 21⅕ secs. Second best time was made by Major Coe (Vauxhall) in the 3-litre class, and third best was Joyce (A.C.) in the 1500-c.c. racing class.

In spite of being superstitious enough to avoid making record-breaking attempts on a Friday, the 13th as a date cannot have worried Thomas, for on that date in September he was placed in each event of the B.A.R.C. Autumn Meeting for which the Leyland-Thomas was entered. Heavy rain up to lunch time had been succeeded by a strong wind which blew with braking effect down the Railway Straight and gave unwanted assistance on the turn by the Vickers shed. The much talked-of duel between the Leyland-Thomas and E.A.D. Eldridge's Fiat was postponed (in point of fact until July 1925) owing to the Fiat, during practice on the Friday, having hit some obstacle which removed its external oil pump. The track was splashingly wet for the 42nd 100-m.p.h. Short Handicap and the 4441-c.c. Sunbeam of R.T.T. Spencer, getting away to a start of 52 seconds, was in front all the way. Swooping from the Banking to the finish in the Railway Straight, Thomas passed P. Rampon's Fiat to finish second. In the third event (27th Lightning Short Handicap) the competitors were reduced to two. Eldridge's Fiat was naturally a non-starter, J.E.P. Howey's Leyland had not been repaired since its crankshaft trouble some time previously and the Lorraine-Dietrich was *hors de combat*. Added to this, the Isotta-Fraschini had some mishap on its way out to the start. So, Thomas was left with only H.W. Cook (Vauxhall) as an opponent, who, although starting 33 seconds ahead and going very well, was unable to prevent the Leyland-Thomas winning fairly easily at 116 m.p.h. In the 41st

100-m.p.h. Long Handicap, Thomas had to give best to the two 3-litre Vauxhalls of Cook and Barclay. Finally Cook and Thomas were at it again in the 27th Lightning Long Handicap after D.R.W. Gedge, driving Le Champion's Isotta-Maybach, had stopped soon after the start. The Vauxhall took a lot of catching and, in fact, led to within 100 yards of the post when the Leyland flashed by to win at an average of 120 m.p.h.

The 200-Miles Race (20th September), which turned out to be an unchallenged, one-two-three win for the team of supercharged Darracqs driven by K. Lee Guinness, G. Duller (who had entered his Thomas Special before being asked to drive a Darracq) and Major H.O.D. Segrave, proved a disastrous event for poor Thomas. His Thomas Special was soon in trouble with faulty ignition due to the valve cover working loose and letting oil run on to the exhaust branches and plugs. Then came a call at the pits for a tyre change and a mechanic managed to let the axle fall off the jack. Thomas's comments, though probably worth hearing, are not recorded. After 30 laps there was more trouble, the description of which can best be taken from *The Autocar's* report which is not only detailed but preserves a certain flavour of the period.

Suddenly came the first really heart-stirring thrill outside the Darracq feats. Parry Thomas was bringing his Special down to the fork at perhaps 90 m.p.h., when his near side front tyre burst, and the car instantaneously attempted to swerve across the track, as if to charge the pits and the crowd behind them. But only for an instant. Quicker than thought, Thomas gripped and held the plunging car, and in a second or two he actually kept it straight one-handed, flinging out his right arm as a warning to another projectile which was close on his tail at the moment. He shot on at practically undiminished speed, pinning the car to as true a course as if it had been on rails. Then the tyre came off. As the car shot up the banking behind the members' hill a second dark object detached itself. "The rim!" we shouted, and we pictured him fighting for life round the corner with his brake drum grinding on the concrete. But in a minute or so round he came again forkwards, still running on the rim. But this furious, tyreless lap at over 70 had stressed the car past bearing, and it began to break up from that moment forwards. As Thomas came in and restarted with his new wheel he got the first real cheer of the afternoon from a huge assembly. Two laps later he shed another tyre, from the off-front wheel this time – the tyres on the car were admittedly much too small.

By three-quarter distance Thomas was running 13th, but by the time the leaders had finished the race the Thomas Special was coming adrift. First the scuttle went overboard and then the exhaust pipe, after flapping about for a lap or two, gave way at the silencer end, pouring its gasses all over R.B. Howey, who was riding as mechanic, until Thomas retired on his 71st lap. In spite of these vicissitudes, it is indeed a compliment to Thomas that he should be singled out for mention as one of the few drivers in the race who set a good example by entering the pit area on the proper side of the black safety line.

On Saturday and Sunday, 4th and 5th October, the Grand Prix de France races for motor cycles and cyclecars, formerly held on a road circuit, took place at the new Montlhéry track to celebrate its official opening. As an additional attraction a six-lap race was arranged between Eldridge's Fiat, Thomas's Leyland-Thomas and an eight-cylindered D'Aoust driven by Arthur Duray. With his mechanics, one of whom was none other than Ken Taylor, Thomas had been at the track during the week and had put in practice laps at around 120 m.p.h. As to the race itself, *The Autocar* reported as follows:

There were more thrills during the last five minutes than in the whole of the two days, when the three big cars, Eldridge's Fiat, J.G.P. Thomas's Leyland and Duray's 8-cylinder D'Aoust ran a six-lap match. The original idea of sending them away together was abandoned and Duray, who made a very bad start, went away first, followed by Thomas and Eldridge at fifteen-second intervals.

On the second round the Leyland passed the D'Aoust easily, for Duray cut out as he entered the bends, and was rarely more than half-way up the banking. On the fourth round the tread of the right-hand rear tyre on the Leyland came off with a report like a pistol, just in front of the timers' box. Thomas, however, did not slacken speed and on the following lap his right rear tyre left the wheel in ribbons, dropping on the track just in front of the pits. Eldridge lost his right rear tread a few seconds after Thomas and at exactly the same spot, the band of rubber shooting up in the air and dropping among the spectators. With no tyre on his right rear wheel, Thomas continued at one hundred miles an hour, to the consternation of the spectators. Eldridge, on the other hand, with only the tread gone, did not slacken speed and brought his Fiat in 200 yards ahead of the Leyland. Time for the 9·3 miles was 4 mins. 37⅘ secs., giving an average of 121·04 m.p.h.; the fastest lap was covered by Thomas in 42⅖ secs. or 131·89 m.p.h. The average speed, in reality, is much higher than the above figures, for the track has been measured very close to the inside edge and the Leyland and the Fiat ran most of the time within a couple of yards of the top of the banking.

Although far from finished, the Montlhéry track is an excellent construction. Undoubtedly faster than Brooklands, it is more dangerous, in the opinion of expert drivers, who state that fast cars have to be forced into and out of the turns.

It is particularly hard on tyres, as is shown by the inability of the Leyland and the Fiat to cover more than three consecutive laps at speed without trouble.

On the Sunday there was another race, this time for cars up to 6 litres, over 10 laps (15½ miles). There was a field of four machines, Pierre de Vizcaya on a Bugatti, Douglas Hawkes with a Ballot, Vladimir de Racowsky with a Peugeot and Thomas with the Leyland-Thomas. In order to reduce the capacity of the Leyland engine, Thomas removed the rockers from the valve gear of the two end cylinders cutting the litreage by 25%. In spite of the handicap of carrying round two passenger cylinders, the Leyland-Thomas finished over half a mile ahead of Vizcaya's Bugatti at an average speed of 111·7 m.p.h. Hawkes came in third and Racowsky fourth.

At the end of the meeting Eldridge made an attempt on his own 10-kilometre record but was unsuccessful. On the same day, the motor racing world was saddened by the news that Count Zborowski had been killed in a crash when driving a new 2-litre supercharged Mercedes in the Italian Grand Prix at Monza. Thomas, as much as anyone, must have felt the loss of this great sportsman.

CHAPTER VII

Racing, 1925

As a result of the cars owned by the late Count Zborowski being offered for sale, Thomas came into possession of the Higham Special. He had been down to Higham to see the car and, having bought it for £125, it was then towed to his workshops at Brooklands. Much work, thought and calculations must have been put in during this year on the redesigning of the monster, although it did not appear in public until the following year.

Another machine was now in course of construction, and this was the first of the 1½-litre straight-eight Thomas Specials – the "flat irons". Thomas wrote:

Some of the Brooklands habitués were, I think, somewhat amused when, after having raced the big Leyland-Thomas for a season, I launched out with my little streamlined 1½-litre "Special". One or two asked me how I liked the change-over from the steady, comfortable Leyland to the small car. I could only reply that handling the one called for a very different method of driving from the other, and an occasional change of mount was always beneficial.

Now that it has been rumoured that I am to appear with a tiny 750-c.c. racer, as well as the 1500-c.c. machine and the small "straight-eight" I intend to drive in the French Grand

68

Prix, I am perhaps better able to explain the points of difference in handling the two types on road and track.

The large car, although faster, is in a sense more easily controlled than the small one, although it certainly calls for much greater physical strength, inasmuch as, being heavier, it does not react so rapidly to outside influences as does the smaller vehicle. Its weight and size tend to make it steadier, while it is certainly more comfortable in just the same way as on a choppy sea a large vessel may be practically unaffected by the heaving waves, while a little boat may be tossed here, there and everywhere.

The light car travelling at 100 m.p.h. or so answers instantaneously to the slightest touch of its controls, which is just as well, because it is affected to a far greater extent, and much more rapidly than its bigger prototype. A bump on the track that would scarcely be noticed in the Leyland may send a little racer shooting off at an unexpected angle. One has, therefore, to be instantly responsive to very rapidly changing conditions; very much more "wide awake" even than when at the wheel of a heavier and faster car.

Another thing is that there is very little sensation of fuss, or effort, on the part of a large engine, as it is turning over less rapidly than is a smaller power unit. Even when "full out" the engine of the Leyland-Thomas is never "revving" at more than 3000 r.p.m. On the other hand, the engine of my little four-cylinder Thomas Special is doing about 4500 r.p.m. when lapping the track at somewhere round about the 100-m.p.h. mark.

Owing to the fact that the smaller engine develops its maximum horsepower at a much higher rate of revolutions, it has not, of course, got the slow-pulling capabilities of the bigger vehicle, which will run as slowly as 12 m.p.h. in top gear. Consequently, when driving the Thomas Special, I have to make very full use of my gearbox, although, of course, I also do so when making a quick getaway on the Leyland.

The new body which I have built for the 1500-c.c. car is modelled on the lines of the one I have used for the Leyland-Thomas, which has proved very successful in overcoming wind resistance. Although very light, being made of thin sheet aluminium stretched over a fuselage of steel tubing, it is so strong and rigid that a man of sufficient physical strength could lift the rear wheels off the ground by putting both hands under the point of the tail and giving a good upward "heave".

I only wish I could shrink to suitable proportions, so that I could make the smaller-engined cars proportionately low and narrow! As it is, my new racing body, although, of course, very short, is about as high as that on the Leyland chassis. It is narrower, naturally, as it is only a single-seater, while in order to give me sufficient room I have had the lower edge of the steering wheel rim cut away. On this little light racer I have kept a central change, with the result that the gear lever comes between my knees. However, this does not matter, as I am only using it for track racing.

Naturally, a small car built for road-racing has to be more robust and provided with excellent brakes. I have therefore designed a little "straight eight" of only 1500 c.c., and supercharged, for the French Grand Prix. Some parts of this chassis are already taking shape, but I anticipate having a very busy time getting it completed in time for the event.

The reason for my Grand Prix car being only 1500 c.c., although competing against 2-litre racing cars, is that the 2-litre racer will, so far as the big international events go, be out of date next year. By running a 1½-litre car I shall be able, no doubt, to gather data which should be valuable in the event of my designing a racing car for the 1926 Grand Prix.

Evidently, the smaller car scores in road events, such as hill-climbs. It is due to its shorter wheelbase and lower weight.

Thomas did not take part in the hill climb at Kop this year but his 4-cylinder Thomas Special and the Leyland-Thomas were entered for races at the B.A.R.C. Easter Meeting. As the Bank Holiday weather turned out to be cold and wet and the rain steadily increased, the stewards seriously considered abandoning the meeting after the second race. It was finally decided, however, to cancel the 100 m.p.h. and the Lightning Short and Long handicaps, the entrants being able to transfer to similar events in the Whitsun programme. The result of all this was that Thomas had one run in Rapson's Lanchester (18th 90-m.p.h. Long Handicap) going well but not securing a place. A cloak of best quality melodrama surrounded a non-starter in the second race. The Nazzaro entered by N.T. Chamberlayne, with whom Thomas was to have a business partnership at a later date, was reported to have been "wilfully damaged during the night by some evilly-disposed persons".

On 25th April, the Surbiton Motor Club provided four events for cars at their Brooklands meeting and Thomas drove in three of them. In the Surbiton Junior Short Handicap, he drove the 4-cylinder Thomas Special. The race was won by Benjafield's Bentley which was followed home by Barclay's Vauxhall, Thomas losing third place to Miss Ivy Cummings' old G.N. driven by Le Champion. In the second race, the smaller Thomas Special driven by D.R.W. Gedge came in second to Barnato's Bugatti. Thomas himself was out again for the Surbiton Junior Long Handicap in his own Thomas Special in competition with his personal friends George Duller (Bugatti) and Mrs. Duller (Amilcar). The trio followed Barclay's Vauxhall past the post, Duller, possibly with more enthusiasm than tact, passing his wife within a few yards of the finish, and Thomas running fourth. The Surrey Lightning Long Handicap was the last event, and for this the Leyland-Thomas was brought to the line together with J.E.P. Howey's Leyland, now with a similarly streamlined body, Lionel Rapson's Lanchester with R.B. Howey at the wheel and L.C. Le Champion's Isotta-Maybach. From scratch Thomas was off to some purpose, easily passing J.E.P. Howey, who was soft pedalling his Leyland, for out of kindness of heart he was carrying a small boy as passenger. The Lanchester took some catching, and, although Thomas achieved this on the last run down the Railway Straight, he had left his final spurt too late to prevent a win by Le Champion.

Early in May, Thomas was staying at the Chateau in Montlhéry, having entered the 4-cylinder Thomas Special for the Grand Prix d'Ouverture to be run on Sunday, 17th. The car was a single-seater with a normal gearbox, the epicyclic gear being removed. Pulling a 3 to 1 top gear, the engine revs did not exceed 4000 r.p.m. There were sixteen starters out of the twenty-eight entrants, two of the non runners being specially prepared 8-cylinder, 1500-c.c. Bugattis. Only one of the cars was brought to the track and that by Ettore Bugatti himself. The car was beautifully turned out, but a short run proved that le Patron's theory that a racing car did not require rear springs (rubber blocks being interposed between axle and frame) was a faulty one and back went the car to Molsheim. Once the race was on, it became obvious that the unsuper-charged 1500-c.c. Talbots driven by Duller, Segrave and Count Conelli were going to be well to the fore. At the end of three laps the order was Segrave, Duller, Thomas, Eldridge (on an Eldridge Special) and Conelli. After 20 laps (about 30 miles) Segrave was still in the lead, averaging 96·4 m.p.h., followed by Duller, Conelli and Thomas, while further to the rear were the Eldridge Special and a second Thomas Special driven by R.C. Morgan. At 100 kilometres the race average had gone up to 98·9 m.p.h. and the three Talbots and Thomas were still on the same lap, with Eldridge, Morgan and de Joncy (Jean Gras) six laps behind.

Segrave burst his off-side rear tyre at about 110 miles and went in to the pits to change both rear wheels (35 secs.). As he left, Thomas came in for under-bonnet investigations and after several more short stops, retired with magneto trouble. By half distance Morgan's Thomas Special was out, too, with a blown gasket.

The fantastic finish was watched by Thomas and Major Callingham as they stood on the track edge near the finishing line. Segrave had slowed down in third place, realising that he could neither lose nor improve his position and having a healthy respect for the wet track, which was made treacherous by sand and clay soil blown across it from the infield. Duller and Conelli came off the West Banking and spurted for the line, some three lengths apart. At the last moment Conelli decided to try to pass, slid on the wet track, hit the outside retaining wall, seriously injuring an official, spun, turned over and crossed the line upside down. Duller finished without knowing what was going on behind him and won at an average of 97·2 m.p.h., having made a non-stop run. Thomas never moved as the inverted car passed close to where he was, remarking afterwards that, under such circumstances, one was as safe standing still as dancing about. Conelli was thrown out and his car finished on its wheels on the inside of the track. He was extremely lucky in sustaining only very superficial head injuries.

Strangely enough Thomas's next race, that for the Brooklands Gold Vase at the B.A.R.C. Whit Monday Meeting, was also marred by a car turning over. The tendency to drive too high on the banking, causing obstruction to faster cars, was becoming acute and worrying both committee men and drivers. The Leyland-Thomas was hampered by some of this unskilled hogging of the track and was only able to make third place.

Rampon's Fiat came in first followed by Kidston's Bugatti. Behind them, Major Coe, coming from the edge of the banking, slid down tail first, swung round and went tail over bonnet on to the grass verge – as a reporter said, "in a cloud of dust and pieces". Almost miraculously neither Coe nor his mechanic was very seriously hurt.

The Brooklands Founders' Gold Cup (5¾ miles) was a win in grand style for Thomas. In the first half lap he had cancelled out the 16-secs. start given to Howey's sister Leyland, and on the second he was past Le Champion's Isotta-Maybach and Barclay's Vauxhall. Kidston's blue Bugatti disappeared behind the hill with the Leyland-Thomas close astern, and it was Thomas's masterly swoop on to the Railway Straight that settled the race in his favour. His win brought him back to "owes 9 seconds" for the 42nd 100-m.p.h. Long Handicap. The Leyland travelled extremely fast as Thomas endeavoured to shake off this ball-and-chain penalty of success, but the score-board showed:

1. Barclay (Vauxhall)
2. Barnato (Bugatti)
3. Thomas (Leyland-Thomas)

He next drove the Lanchester in the 19th 90-m.p.h. Long Handicap but was not in the first three. Then came the closing event (28th Lightning Long Handicap), an easy race to follow as there were only three runners. Rehandicapped to "owes 6 seconds", the Leyland-Thomas left the line 42 secs. behind R.B. Howey driving the 5-litre Ballot. Douglas Hawkes had been first away (56 secs.) on the Lanchester, but his car was misfiring and he was left behind after one lap. Breaking the lap record at 129·36 m.p.h. on the second time round, Thomas came within striking distance of the Ballot. On the final lap, the Leyland went past, high on the Home Banking, and won at 119·4 m.p.h.

On Sunday, 7th June, there was racing at Montlhéry again and the chief attraction was a race over 9·3 miles between a 12-cylinder Delage in the hands of Albert Divo, the Leyland-Thomas, Eldridge's Fiat and something called a Bogenschutz Special, which had a chassis of unknown make fitted with an 180-h.p. Hispano-Suiza aeroplane engine. Divo won the race with the Delage, averaging 125·5 m.p.h. and breaking the lap record (previously held by Thomas at 135·07 m.p.h.) with a speed of 136·3 m.p.h. The Leyland-Thomas was second and Eldridge's Fiat third.

The B.A.R.C. Summer Meeting, which took place on Saturday, 27th June, was a successful one from the point of view of the racing, the handicapping and the fact that the slower cars were much better behaved on the banking. Attendance figures, however, were lower due partly to an overcast sky and a cold wind, and partly to competition from Wimbledon, Sandown Park and the Hendon Air Pageant.

The early starters disputed the race among themselves in the 44th 100-m.p.h. Short Handicap and the first three to finish were Ropner (Vauxhall), Harvey (Alvis) and Benjafield (Bentley). Coming up from the rear but not in the money were R.B. Howey driving his white Ballot and Thomas, having a try in J.E.P. Howey's car, now officially referred to as a Leyland-Thomas. For the 29th Lightning Short Handicap, Thomas was in his own Leyland-Thomas but although the car ran fast and faultlessly he was not placed in this race either, success being deferred until later in the meeting. W.D. Hawkes, the limit man, went extremely well with his Lorraine-Dietrich, "Vieux Charles", and was in front all the way. R.B. Howey brought the Ballot up from further back to take second place. Although the limit car, this time A. Lanfranchi's Alfa Romeo, won again in the 43rd 100-m.p.h. Long Handicap, it was a near thing. The Alfa was all but caught on the line by Harvey's F.W.D. Alvis which had started 37 secs. later.

Thomas again drove Howey's Leyland-Thomas and this time surged past the four other cars in the race to take third place, close on the undriven rear wheels of the Alvis. Much was expected of Raymond Mays' supercharged A.C. as the cars lined up for the 20th 90-m.p.h. Handicap. Most disappointingly it blew up on the first lap and the leaders were Barclay, driving Lanfranchi's Alfa Romeo, and Barnato (Bentley), both of whom had passed the Horstman driven by H.W. Purdy. The Lanchester, in Thomas's hands, left the scratch mark and proceeded to creep up to the other end of the race. On the last lap it passed the Bentley on the Home Banking and Thomas turned on everything as the angular machine swept down the Railway Straight to pip the Alfa Romeo by little more than a couple of yards and win at 98·5 m.p.h. The 29th Lightning Long Handicap resulted in a much applauded win for Thomas in the Leyland-Thomas No. 1 at the high average speed of 120·15 m.p.h. After watching John Cobb (driving Warde's Fiat), Ellison (Lorraine-Dietrich) and R.B. Howey (Ballot) leave the starting line, Thomas began to get down to business. By lap 2, Howey was in front and the Leyland streaked down the Railway Straight to pass the Fiat and the Lorraine-Dietrich on the Byfleet Banking. On the last lap Thomas was up with Howey, going in front just after the two cars passed under the Members' Bridge.

The somewhat hastily constructed programme for the West Kent Club's Brooklands Meeting on Saturday, 11th July, had to include two half-mile races to string out the proceedings. Nevertheless, one race during the afternoon more than made up for deficiencies and was to be perhaps one of the most famous contests in the history of Brooklands track. This was the often postponed match between Thomas's Leyland-Thomas and Eldridge's huge Fiat, allegedly for a wager of £500 (20).

Rather a long wait on the starting line served to raise the already tense atmosphere as the red 300-h.p. 21,714-c.c. Fiat and the white and blue 40-h.p. 7266-c.c. Leyland-Thomas stood side by side at the mile box on the Railway Straight. Then the starting bell announced that they were off and, contrary to expectation, the Leyland-Thomas drew ahead. Before the Byfleet Banking was reached, Eldridge took the lead, his Fiat still accelerating and quite obviously taking a great deal of holding on the Banking. As he came out of the turn on to the gradually flattening track, his car started a series of wild swerves. Knowing that he could not afford to let up, with great daring Eldridge headed the still slithering monster on to the Home Banking. By the end of the first lap the Fiat had gained a considerable lead although Thomas, maintaining complete control of the Leyland, was streaking across the concrete astern. Passing the Fork for a second time, the Fiat was steadier but Thomas was creeping up. He made a bid to pass on the Banking but his car slid downwards and he abandoned the attempt. As the two cars tore down the Railway Straight spectators were amazed to see that Eldridge was unable to draw away from his rival. A slight misjudgement on the Byfleet Banking caused the Fiat to broadside in a cloud of dust and, skidding again at the Fork, Eldridge was aware that there was a car behind wanting to pass. Being a true sportsman, he lifted his foot enough to pull well over to allow Thomas room to go ahead should he be able to do so. In a flash the white and blue car was past him and on to the Home Banking. As he followed, Eldridge lost a rear tyre tread while Thomas, more dangerously still, lost a front one. There was no catching the Leyland-Thomas now and it flashed across the line a winner, having put the lap record up to 129·70 m.p.h. and averaging for the race 123·23 m.p.h. The Fiat's best lap was 125·45 m.p.h. and its average 121·19 m.p.h. Calm and faultless judgement allied to the superb behaviour of his car had enabled Thomas to defeat the great power and acceleration so daringly exploited by his opponent. While the two drivers smilingly shook hands and exchanged congratulations, some of the more knowledgeable habitués wiped beads of perspiration from their brows.

Almost immediately after this famous race the Fiat was bought by L.C.G.M. Le Champion who agreed that, should the return match between Eldridge and Thomas be staged during the B.A.R.C. August Meeting, he would put the car at the disposal of its former owner. The August Meeting did not, however, include such an event. The big attraction this time was the inclusion of a 100-mile race.

One of the disappointments of the meeting was that the entry of a new type Invicta, having a four-cylinder F.A.S.T. (Fabbrica Automobili Sport Torino) engine, to be driven by Thomas, did not make its appearance. However, the first race (35th 75-m.p.h. Short Handicap) had its excitements and was won by A.E. Moss's Frontenac-Ford, which had a modified Indianapolis chassis and overhead valves. Having broken an oil pipe which proceeded to pour oil on to the exhaust pipe, the car passed the winning post reasonably well alight. Driving his Thomas Special, Thomas was in competition with another car having a similar engine. This was the Aston Martin, "Green Pea", which was appearing for the first time fitted with a Hooker-Thomas engine. In spite of keeping low on the banking and, in fact, passing below some of the field, Thomas was not able to gain a place. In the 13th Lightning Short Handicap, Le Champion tried out his new acquisition, the big Fiat, though he wisely treated it with great respect. The "smaller" Fiat (10,087 c.c.) driven by John Cobb won, followed home by R.B. Howey driving his brother's Leyland. The Leyland-Thomas No. 1 took fourth place behind J.D. Barclay's Vauxhall.

When Vernon Balls led off with his Amilcar in the 35th 75-m.p.h. Long Handicap he was followed by A. Whale's Calthorpe and four Austin Sevens. Behind them came Scriven's Felix, Malcolm Campbell's 3321-c.c. Chrysler and Thomas in the Thomas Special. Still in the lead on the third lap, the Amilcar was passed by Campbell as they came off the Home Banking. Swooping down to the Railway Straight in what was by now considered as typical Thomas style, the little Thomas Special ran through to win at 96·75 m.p.h. Starting 5 secs. ahead of a larger engined Bugatti driven by L. Preston in the 44th 100-m.p.h. Long Handicap, Thomas worked the Lanchester solemnly through a field which included a Grand Prix Napier, the Halford Special, a 2-litre Austro-Daimler, an Austin Seven and two Alvises. Thomas won at 98·75 m.p.h., at the same time as a fire, which had broken out in the Paddock House, was extinguished by the fire brigade.

The 30th Lightning Long Handicap proved to be a thrilling duel between Barclay's Vauxhall and Hawkes' Lorraine-Dietrich. The scrap went on throughout the race while the Leylands of Howey and Thomas worked their way up from 35 seconds and scratch respectively. At the end, the Leylands took the lead, Thomas being unable to overcome Howey's initial advantage and Barclay gained third place with the Vauxhall.

Now came the 100-Miles Handicap. Three interesting cars were non-starters: the 1921 straight-eight Grand Prix Sunbeam, a new single-seater Talbot and the Eldridge Special which, having been brought all the way from Montlhéry, broke a con-rod in the paddock. As the cars were flagged away, E.C. Gordon England showed a remarkable turn of speed, making the most of his handicap. A. Waite's Austin was soon in trouble, as was the Marendaz Special. Thomas was away with the 1847-c.c. Thomas Special (7 mins. 50 secs.), 47 secs. ahead of Barnato's 3-litre Bentley, and he made good progress right from the start. At quarter distance the order was Gordon England (Austin), Dunfee (Salmson), Douglas (Aston Martin), Purdy (Alvis) and Thomas (Thomas Special). Behind them, the two Bentleys of Benjafield and Barnato and the Vauxhall driven by Barclay fought a battle of their own. The first four cars were in the same positions when the race was half-way through. At three-quarter distance, the Austin, though still leading, was visibly slowing and the Aston Martin had moved into second place. Thomas was now third and Dunfee fourth. A lap later the Thomas Special was second, and three laps later it led the field. Having built up a comfortable lead, Thomas was first over the line averaging 98·23 m.p.h. Second came Douglas' Aston Martin (88·94 m.p.h.) and third Barnato (Bentley) who had averaged 96·43 m.p.h. Thomas's well-earned victory was greeted with much cheering from the crowd.

Sometime in the middle of August, the Leyland-Thomas was shipped to Boulogne for the Speed Trials which, this year, were organised jointly by the French authorities and the Essex Motor Club. Thomas had entered, as before, for the two speed tests and the hill climb which were scheduled for Thursday, 27th August, but disaster overtook him during practice. Skidding on the wet tarmac road, the Leyland-Thomas slewed on to the grass verge, smashed into a tree stern first and finished up on the road again with the body wrecked and the back axle gaping open. The impact with the tree must have been considerable as Thomas had difficulty in getting out of the cockpit which had partially closed up like some giant mouth, and he considered himself lucky to suffer no more than a badly bruised leg. The propeller shaft had been driven forward to such an extent that the crankshaft had been dislodged and the main bearing housings in the crankcase were broken.

Reviewing the pieces, back at his own workshop, Thomas realised that the chassis and engine would have to be scrapped and a new car built using odd parts from the old car where these proved undamaged and suitable.

With no Leyland-Thomas of his own available for the rest of the year, Thomas made use of his Thomas Special and the Rapson Lanchester at the B.A.R.C. Autumn Meeting on 12th September. It was a beautiful day for that time of the year, and added interest was given to the meeting by the fact that some of the cars specially prepared for the coming 200-Miles Race were being given trial runs in various events. One such was R.C. Morgan's Thomas Special which had already distinguished itself at Boulogne by getting a first and a second place.

After witnessing a dead-heat in the first race between Turner's Austro-Daimler and Purdy's Alvis (the second in the history of Brooklands), Thomas took over Capt. J.E.P. Howey's Leyland-Thomas for the 31st Lightning Short Handicap, Howey himself driving his Ballot. Kaye Don made the running in the Wolseley Viper but was overtaken by Cobb (Fiat), Thomas getting the Leyland-Thomas into third place quite comfortably. For the 45th 100-m.p.h. Long Handicap, Howey took his Leyland back and Thomas turned out in the Lanchester. They were matched against Barnato (Bentley), Cushman (Crossley), and Campbell (Sunbeam). Thomas was soon past Campbell, while astern the Leyland seemed held back by an attack of popping and banging. The trouble, whatever it was, soon cleared and Howey streaked away to make the only scratch win of the day with Thomas's Lanchester second and Barnato's Bentley third. This was Thomas's best placing for the day in spite of being entered for six events (in two of these Thomas's performance was not even mentioned by the reporters). He may possibly have been feeling the strain of his crash at Boulogne but it was certainly not one of his good days. Some trouble detained the Thomas Special in the paddock and Thomas was late getting out to the start for the 21st 90-m.p.h. Long Handicap. The fault must have been persistent for he drove back again looking rather disconsolate. For the last race (31st Lightning Long Handicap) Thomas had the wheel of Howey's Leyland-Thomas once more while its owner turned out with the Ballot, the engine of which had required considerable attention after its previous race. The line up was:

	Handicap
Benjafield (Bentley)	47 secs.
Barclay (Vauxhall)	39 secs.
Howey (Ballot)	25 secs.
Cobb (Fiat)	18 secs.
Thomas (Leyland)	scratch

After one lap the Vauxhall led with Howey second. By the third lap Howey was in front, Barclay finishing second and Thomas third.

There was to have been an Amilcar for Thomas to drive in the 200-Miles Race on 26th September, but before the race day this was scratched, together with a similar car to have been driven by C. Libovitch. Watching the race, as he unquestionably did, Thomas's main interest would have been in R.C. Morgan's Hooker-Thomas-engined Aston Martin which put up a good show, reaching 3rd place for a time but being put out by carburetter trouble after 49 laps.

On 2nd October the Essex Motor Club held their final meeting at the track and, needless to say, Thomas was there. He was quite plainly amusing himself in one of the 8½-mile races when he drove Howey's Ballot, starting 6 secs. ahead of Howey (Leyland-Thomas), who was past him on the first lap. Taking no risks with a car strange to him, Thomas was not in the first three. Later in the afternoon there was a 50-miles race and for this Thomas entered the Thomas Special. The event was won by Duller with an Austin Seven and there is no comment upon Thomas's fortunes in the race.

Thus ended Thomas's racing season for 1925, satisfactory and successful except for the one bad accident of his whole career which destroyed the Leyland-Thomas into which he had put so much work.

CHAPTER VIII

Racing, 1926

During the early months of the year Thomas's workshops at Brooklands must have been an impressive sight. By then, the results of intense work during the winter were taking shape. The Higham Special which Thomas had had in his possession for a whole year was now finalised. A Leyland radiator had been fitted enclosed by a cowl much on the lines of the Leyland-Thomas, which encased the front dumb irons. The twelve-cylinder Liberty engine now had four Zenith carburetters, two at each end of the manifolding which lay between the blocks of cylinders. With pistons specially designed by himself, the engine developed between 500 and 600 b.h.p. at 2000 r.p.m. The Benz gearbox had been retained but was now linked to the engine by a Thomas clutch. The blunt tail of the Higham Special was at first retained, with no head fairing, although it was not long before Thomas altered this to the lower, longer and more pointed version with fairings before and behind the driver's head so characteristic of his cars (33). The car was actually completed towards the end of April and although the time was 9 p.m. and it was quite dark, Thomas's enthusiasm was such that he insisted on being push-started (the second attempt was a success) and drove twice round his worksheds.

The car was rechristened "Babs". It is not possible, after the passage of so much time, to say exactly why Thomas chose the name. One explanation has it that a mechanic had chalked the word "Baby" on the huge engine and that this appealed to Thomas's sense of humour, as it quite likely would have done. Alternatively, "Babs" being the popular nickname of many young ladies in the nineteen-twenties, there were probably several low-waisted and cloche-hatted reasons from which one could choose. Again, Thomas's love of children may equally easily have provided the answer; a particular possibility here being his own little niece Pamela.

The second major undertaking in the workshops was the reconstruction of the Leyland-Thomas wrecked at Boulogne, and by the end of March the car was almost ready. Work was also going forward on the construction of the 1½-litre straight-eight Thomas Specials, two of which were eventually made. A third chassis existed in embryo and this may have been intended for the 750-c.c. car which was never made. A press report as early as December 1925 mentions that three cars were being constructed and had already reached a fairly advanced stage. It is possible that Thomas intended to have a third car with a 1½-litre engine and to change the power unit for a 750-c.c. one when this should come off the drawing board. The reporter, however, cannot have been very reliably informed about the "fairly advanced stage" of the third car. Design had begun early in 1925 when it was hoped to run one in the French Grand Prix that year but so far, no car had appeared. The machines were now progressing, and furthermore it was announced in March that the entries for the Duke of York's Trophy motor-boat races (to take place on the Thames between Mortlake and Putney at the end of June) were expected to include one from "Mr. J.G.P. Thomas with a Thomas eight-cylinder super-charged engine". This boat, however, never materialised. Barnato and Eyston were also racing boats of their own. To round off the winter's work J.E.P. Howey's Leyland had received attention and now had cylinder bores of 95 mm. instead of 89 mm.

(Left to right) Thomas, Major Callingham and Lt.-Cdr. Mackenzie-Grieve stand by Major Callingham's 30-98 h.p. Vauxhall outside "The Hermitage" at Brooklands.

Thomas at the wheel of the Leyland-Thomas No. 1.

"Babs" with her bonnet removed to show the 27-litre, 12-cylinder Liberty engine. Standing behind the car *(left to right)* are Major Calling-ham, Mr. Harold Parker, a mechanic and Thomas.

An R.A.C. official inspecting "Babs" in her Pendine garage, while Thomas, wearing his well-known Fair Isle pullover, stands by.

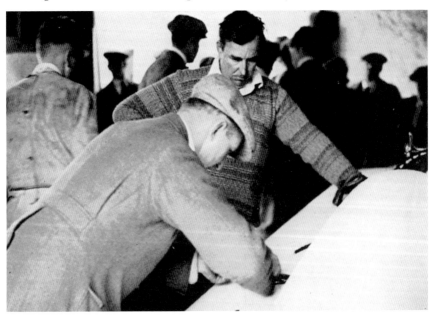

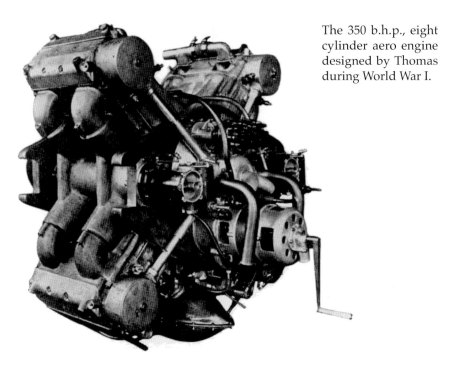

The 350 b.h.p., eight cylinder aero engine designed by Thomas during World War I.

The first Leyland Eight engine to be built showing the 3-piece cylinder head which was afterwards discarded. The three reservoir tanks for petrol, engine oil and gear oil are seen on the scuttle.

Above:The Leyland Eight short "Speed Model" chassis used for the open cars. The stout radius rods to the front axle can be seen.

Opposite: Offside view of the short chassis Leyland Eight showing the rear-spring-operated chassis lubricator. The servo-brake pedal is almost hidden by the hand brake lever.

Below:Thomas at the wheel of the Leyland Eight four-seater tourer.

The two-seater Leyland Eight, stripped for racing, as it first appeared at Brooklands in 1922.

Capt. J.E.P. Howey watches Thomas making adjustments to the Leyland at Brooklands in August 1923.

The 1493-c.c. Marlborough-Thomas sports car as shown at Olympia in the Motor Show of 1923. The car is identical with the 200 Miles Race car except for the addition of flared wings.

The Marlborough-Thomas car in racing trim with the bonnet removed to show the o.h.c. Hooker-Thomas engine. Thomas's passenger is Kenneth Thomson.

The 1493-c.c., four-cylinder Hooker-Thomas-engined Thomas Special first run at Brooklands in 1924. Its lines show a similarity to those of the big Leyland-Thomas in its final form.

The Leyland competing in the Speed Trials at Southsea in August 1922.

Thomas (Marlborough-Thomas) making an ascent of Kop Hill in 1923.

11th July 1923. The Leyland, with its first racing body, during the unsuccessful attempt on the Double Twelve Hour record, cooling its tyres in water supplied by fire hoses.

11th July 1925. The Leyland-Thomas No. 1 gets away to a good start in the famous match race with Eldridge's 300-h.p. Fiat.

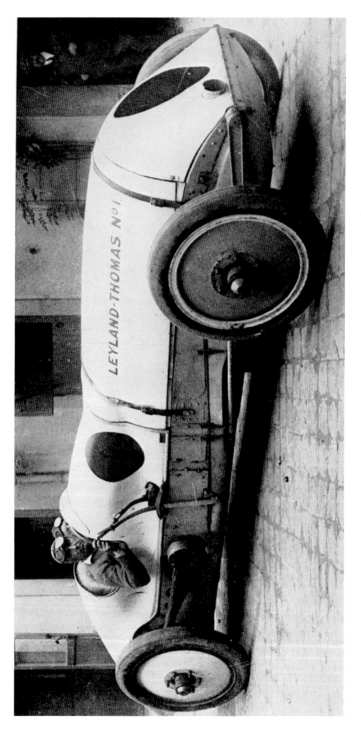

Thomas, with Reid Railton as passenger, in the Leyland-Thomas No. 1 outside the Chateau at Montlhéry.

1926. Thomas in one of the two 1½-litre, straight-eight "flat iron" Thomas Specials.

Left: Head-on view of the "flat-iron" Thomas Special.

Below: The 1½-litre, straight-eight engine.

Thomas's stable of cars. "Babs" in her final form is on the left of the picture flanked by the Leyland-Thomas No. 1 and the straight-eight Thomas Special.

The 6178-c.c. Lanchester, owned by P. Lionel Rapson, which Thomas drove many times in races at Brooklands and with which he broke a number of records.

The Higham Special as purchased by Thomas after Count Zborowski's death.

"Babs" (ex-Higham Special), in her first form with rounded tail, making her first World's Record attempt on Pendine Sands (October 1925).

Above: "Babs" at Brooklands before the successful attempt on the Land Speed Record at Pendine in April 1926. The forward facing air intakes for the carburetters (later removed) can be seen above the radiator cowl.

Opposite: "Babs" passing through the measured mile on Pendine Sands in April 1926 when Thomas became the holder of the World's Land Speed Record, achieving an average of 171·09 m.p.h. for the kilometre and of 170·624 m.p.h. for the mile.

Below: "Babs" with improved body and long tail running at Brooklands in 1926.

Thomas driving "Babs" on to the sands at Pendine for the last time, on the occasion of the ill-fated record attempt.

The wrecked car.

The first meeting of the year at Brooklands was the B.A.R.C. Easter Meeting on 4th April. The weather was glorious, the crowd much larger than usual and there was a successful innovation in the form of a limit line painted on the track ten feet from the top edge of the banking.

The 47th 100-m.p.h. Short Handicap showed that the handicappers were feeling their way at the commencement of a new season, for A. Goutte's Salmson established a lead of nearly a mile in the two laps. Thomas had brought out the new Leyland-Thomas, hurriedly prepared and lacking its tail, to see how it went. He had not expected it to have, as yet, a comparable performance to the previous car but, although he completed the race, all was not well and he scratched the car from the only other race for which it was entered (32nd Lightning Long Handicap). The Lanchester was entered for two races and Thomas, although starting from scratch in the 22nd 90-m.p.h. Long Handicap, had Goutte's Salmson behind him at "owes 21 seconds". This seemingly heavy extra penalty on the French car proved to be just as Goutte almost caught the winning Bentley, driven by Barnato, on the line. Thomas was not able to manage a place. Conditions were more favourable in the 46th 100-m.p.h. Long Handicap and Thomas was able to secure his only win of the day. At first the lead was taken by Turner's Austro-Daimler but the back-markers were soon coming up. From scratch, Barclay's Vauxhall passed Thomas in the Lanchester (12 secs.) and was closing on Barnato's Bentley and Meeson's Vauxhall. On lap 2 the leaders were Meeson followed by Barnato, while Barclay and Thomas were close astern. Then came misjudgement and near-catastrophe. On the last lap, Thomas saw his chance and, keeping well down on the banking, passed below the other three cars. Barclay, on the other hand, decided that he would pass high up and nearly hit the tail of Meeson's car. Under heavy braking, Barclay went perilously near the edge and then in a cloud of dust the Vauxhall, at right angles to the track, slid to the bottom of the banking. Thomas won at an average of exactly 100 m.p.h. with Barnato and Meeson behind him.

By the time it came to the B.A.R.C. Whitsun Meeting (24th May) Thomas was already the holder of the world's land speed record. The fact that "Babs" was entered for three races drew an even larger Bank Holiday crowd than usual. The third race of the meeting was the Brooklands Gold Vase Handicap (5¾ miles) and the world record breaker made its first track appearance. Contrary to the printed programme and causing chaos among the bookies, Thomas let John Cobb drive "Babs" and took the wheel of the Lanchester himself, the handicaps being left as they were. As it turned out, the race was won by Capt. A.G. Miller's 4890-c.c. Sunbeam and neither Cobb nor Thomas were in the money. Cobb showed admirable discretion by treating the crowd (and himself) to a spectacular get-away along the Railway Straight and then soft pedalling sufficiently to keep "Babs" well under control.

For the 33rd Lightning Long Handicap, Thomas drove "Babs", Cobb took the Leyland-Thomas and R.B. Howey was in his brother's Leyland. The two Vauxhalls of Barclay and Meeson made up the field. Meeson led off at 48 seconds, Barclay at 30 seconds and then followed what might be called "Thomas's brood". "Babs" was past the two Leylands in no time and in due course overhauled Meeson's Vauxhall. The limitations of the track, however, prevented the use of sufficient speed to catch Barclay and Thomas had to be content with second place. The last race of the meeting was "The Star" Gold Star Handicap and for this Cobb again drove "Babs" and Thomas took the Leyland-Thomas. In the line-up were R.B. Howey (Ballot), Campbell (Bugatti), Barclay (Vauxhall) and Miller (Sunbeam). Having had three laps in which to reshuffle themselves the order across the line was Howey, Thomas and then Campbell.

Being now so much engrossed in record breaking, Thomas quite obviously did not take the B.A.R.C. Summer Meeting (3rd July) very seriously. He scratched the Leyland-Thomas which was entered for the final "Lightning Long" race and took over the driving of the Rapson-entered Lanchester, whereupon the car's handicap was increased. Thomas drove it in the 48th 100-m.p.h. Long Handicap achieving no success, but in the 24th 90-m.p.h. Long Handicap the Lanchester came in first, with F.B. Halford's 1496-c.c. Halford all but counteracting the 26 seconds it had given to its 6178-c.c. competitor at the start.

August Bank Holiday (2nd August) was a day of perfect motor-racing weather and the B.A.R.C. August Meeting was a well-attended and altogether successful event. For the 35th Lightning Short Handicap, Thomas was on scratch with "Babs" (which appeared on the programme as "Thomas Special, 26,907 c.c.") and to his left in the line-up was a formidable array of fast cars: R.B. Howey's Ballot, a 4890-c.c. Sunbeam driven by Kaye Don, Barclay's Vauxhall and George Duller's 1990-c.c. Bugatti, which had the largest handicap (31 seconds). For most of the race there was a serious tussle between the Bugatti, the Vauxhall and the Sunbeam. Towards the end of the second lap the order was Sunbeam, Bugatti, Vauxhall with "Babs" closing rapidly. On the Home Banking "Babs" was third and then came the "Thomas swoop" on to the Railway Straight and Duller found himself third although the Sunbeam was far enough in front not to be overtaken. Driving the Leyland-Thomas in the 49th 100-m.p.h. Long Handicap, Thomas had the benefit of the extra lap and a car more suited to the track, and he used these advantages to turn the tables on Kaye Don in the Sunbeam, albeit at the very last moment. A new Rover, driven by E. Poppe, scored its first placing in a race by coming third, Thomas's winning average was 117·88 m.p.h. and the event was won by 15 yards.

Duller and Barclay were again in competition with the Leyland-Thomas in the 35th Lightning Long Handicap, and in addition there were Barnato with a Bugatti and Don with the Wolseley Viper. Thomas ran away with the race, finishing 100 yards ahead of Duller's Bugatti, at an average of 116·96 m.p.h., the third man being Barclay whose Vauxhall had started on level terms (41 secs.) with Duller.

To finish off the meeting in an original manner, there was the *Evening News* 100-Miles Handicap. The race was made even more unusual by the fact that Thomas was driving Barclay's 3-litre Vauxhall. The field was large and engine sizes varied from Waite's supercharged 750-c.c. Austin to the Bentleys of Barnato and Benjafield and the Sunbeam driven by J.S. Spenser. Trouble, mostly from tyres, eliminated nearly half the entry in a very short time but out in front a Salmson-Amilcar battle was in progress. First Dunfee (Salmson) led Vernon Balls (Amilcar) and Hazelhurst (Salmson). Then Balls led until he had to go in to change a plug, getting back as far as third place by 16 laps. By this time, Waite's Austin had taken the lead but clutch slip after four more laps ended this challenge, Dunfee resuming first place. By the following lap, the two Bugattis of Eyston and Douglas had come to the front. Oil starvation eliminated Eyston who had been confidently turning on the tap of his reserve oil tank without knowing that the pipe had fractured and that he was lubricating the track. The final result was a win for Capt. Douglas's almost standard Type 37 Bugatti at 94·75 m.p.h. Second came Jack Dunfee (1087-c.c. Salmson) at 81·41 m.p.h. and third Thomas on the Vauxhall, who had established a new Class E 100-mile record at 104·82 m.p.h., in spite of losing the tread from one rear tyre.

The next feature at Brooklands was the British Grand Prix on 7th August. The list of entries showed that two of the new 8-cylinder, 1½-litre Thomas Specials (23, 24) were down to run, one,

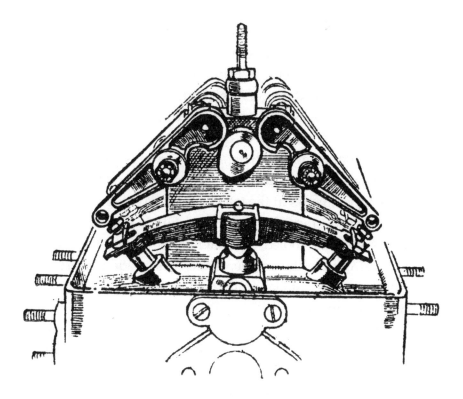

Figure 3. Diagram 8-cylinder Thomas Special: central camshaft and leaf spring operated valves

supercharged (Thistlethwayte's), against the name of R.C. Gallop, while the unblown version was to be driven by Thomas himself. *The Autocar* provided the following interesting information:

The first Thomas Special, which is the property of T. Thistlethwayte, is almost complete. The second, which is for J.G.P. Thomas himself, is very far from ready when one considers that the race is as near as the first week of next month. Both cars have ingenious chassis distinctly in the Thomas manner. The engines are straight-eights of 52 by 88 mm., bore and stroke, cylinder barrels and jackets being of aluminium with steel liners for the pistons. There is a detachable head, and in place of the connecting rod and eccentric drive for the camshaft, a train of spur gears has been employed. The valves, of which there are two to each cylinder, have the typical leaf spring of the Thomas design (22), and the same type of operating mechanism as the Leylands. Both engines have plain bearings, though the white metal used is not the same in each case, and both have a Roots supercharger at the front end of the crankcase.

In this respect there is an unusual point in that the superchargers are water cooled, the water passing round the inside of the casing from the engine, while, as is modern practice, the supercharger sucks from the carburetter instead of blowing through it.

As the engine is high relative to the frame, though low relative to the ground, a separate water tank is fitted in the scuttle to maintain sufficient head for the radiator, which is inclined backwards at a sharp angle. For the lubrication a separate pump is employed, the crankcase being scavenged by a second oil pump. The very ingenious fabric multi-plate clutch which Thomas has used with success for some time is naturally embodied in this design, and behind the clutch there is only a single universal joint.

The gearbox mechanism is interesting because the gear lever movement from first to second involves the passage of the lever through the gate, yet the change from third to top entails another movement through the gate so that the path of the lever would be drawn as an X. To anyone except the designer-driver, this would seem likely to introduce considerable difficulties.

The frame is underslung (28), the engine and other components, therefore, being maintained at their proper height by brackets. The purpose of dropping the frame to this

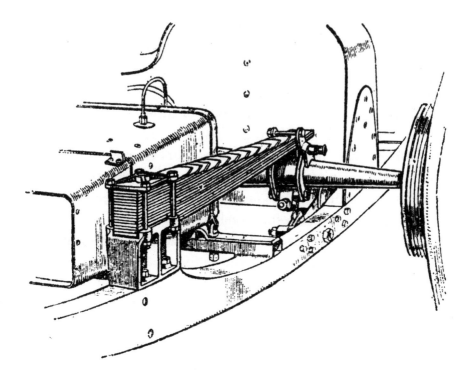

Figure 4. Diagram 8-cylinder Thomas Special: rear axle and suspension

extent is to bring the position of the driving seat much lower than usual; the centre of gravity of the car, in fact, is extremely low. All four brakes are operated by the pedal, but can be actuated also by the hand lever, which, again in accordance with Thomas's usual custom, pushes forward instead of pulling back.

Further details can be gleaned from *The Motor* which says:

As the minimum weight for Grand Prix racers has been increased for next year, there is no longer the same need to cut down weight to the utmost. Consequently, Mr. Thomas has decided to take full advantage of the superior rigidity of a cast-iron crankcase, as compared with one made of aluminium. Large inspection plates permit of easy examination of the big end bearings.

The cylinders are separate units, of cast-iron, and fit into aluminium jackets, which are cast in pairs. The head is of cast-iron, with all the combustion chambers machined to a perfect hemispherical form and provided with two tulip valves per cylinder. The joint between the cylinders and the head is a copper-asbestos washer, while rubber and linen rings separate the head and water jackets. This arrangement allows for the expansion of the cylinders and water jackets when the engine reaches normal running temperature. ...

The rockers are of large size, as indeed are most of the parts of the engine. The Thomas Special power unit is, in effect, what Strickland would term "a large engine with small cylinders". It is hoped to get a speed of some 6500 r.p.m. and this naturally necessitates large bearings and a relatively heavy crankshaft. ...

The clutch, which is of the multi-disc type and only about 3½ ins. in diameter, consists of a large number of die-pressed Ferodo plates, from the edges of which the drive is taken direct, and steel plates. A massive spherical universal joint, supported in a phosphor-bronze housing, transmits the power to the gearbox, which is mounted on the forward end of the torque tube. Giving four forward speeds and reverse, the box is designed on very robust lines, all gears being of large dimensions. The constant-mesh pinions are at the back. The back axle is of unorthodox design and very interesting, but we are not at present permitted to divulge the secret of its design. Let it suffice that it is of the fully floating type, the driving shafts being of very substantial dimensions.

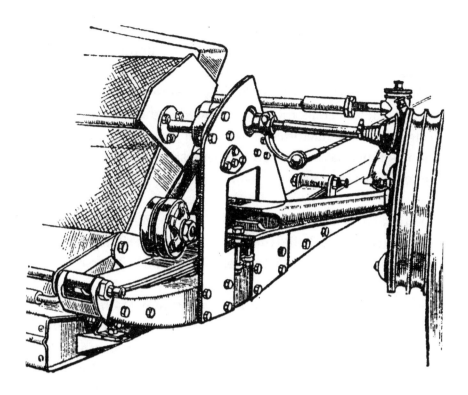

Figure 5. 8-cylinder Thomas Special: front axle and brake layout

The chassis frames, constructed by Messrs. Rubery, Owen & Co., resemble sledges, for the dumb-irons curve upwards at each end. The whole frame thus passes under both axles while the driver's seat is a steel cross-member measuring about 20 ins. from back to front, placed at a height of only 5 ins. from the ground. Owing to the chassis design, the front axle, which is equipped with brakes of the Perrot type, is dropped much less than usual (29). The frame is curved so as to provide a perfectly streamlined foundation for the body, while the bottom of the vehicle will be perfectly flat and parallel to the ground.

The cars, which had steel bodies for the sole purpose of increasing the chassis weight to a figure above the minimum allowed, weighed, with fuel, oil and water on board, about 1700 lb.

Owing to gearbox troubles both cars were unfortunately non-starters. However, as the race included eight-cylinder 1½-litre designs from the factories of Talbot, Delage, Bugatti and Alvis, Thomas must have watched the contest with more than usual interest. The result was:

1. Delage (Senechal & Wagner)   71·61 m.p.h.
2. Bugatti (Campbell)   68·82 m.p.h.
3. Delage (Benoist & Dubonnet)   68·12 m.p.h.

The track was taken on the following Saturday (14th August) by the Essex Motor Club for their Brooklands meeting which included events for both cars and motor cycles. Thomas was there with the Leyland-Thomas, but in the first race in which he took part, the white and blue car was seen to come slowly off the Byfleet Banking during the third lap and coast towards Thomas's sheds. The trouble cannot have been serious for the car was ready on the scratch mark for the very next race (Essex Lightning Long Handicap) alongside Miller's 5-litre Sunbeam driven by Kaye Don (32 secs.), and Malcolm Campbell's 2-litre Bugatti (37 secs.). It took two laps for these three to catch up with the field and on the third Thomas was past Don on the Railway Straight while Campbell was making easy work of the rest of the field on the Byfleet Banking. With the Leyland streaking after him, Campbell managed to get home by 60 yards, Thomas taking second place with his off-side rear tyre shredded on the inside and worn right down on the outside. The fifth event was the Winners' Handicap, open to those gaining first or second places in the previous three races, and in this event Thomas was able to beat Campbell who had three seconds less start that he had had in the race before. Neither of them, however, were able to prevent G.N. Norris (Lea-Francis) getting in first, 50 yards ahead of them. As a final "bonne bouche", a cars versus motor cycles handicap was arranged between the two fastest cars and the two fastest motor cycles over 8¾ miles. The following detailed version of the race appeared in *The Motor*:

As it transpired this event provided the most thrilling finish of the day. J.G. Parry Thomas (Leyland-Thomas) and Capt. M. Campbell (Bugatti) being matched against the two fastest motorcycles, an 8-h.p. Zenith ridden by H.J. Knight and a single-cylinder 3½-h.p. Grindlay-Peerless ridden by C.W.G. Lacey. Thomas was, of course, on scratch and Campbell also had to concede a considerable start to both motorcycles. For two laps Lacey held a useful lead from Knight, although Campbell and Thomas had gained very considerably. Campbell caught and passed the Zenith rider half-way down the Railway Straight in the final lap and then set out in pursuit of Lacey, whom he overtook on the Byfleet Banking. In the meantime, Thomas had also closed up with the motorcycles, and coming off the banking to the Fork, he attempted to pass Knight. The motorcyclist, however, was going so fast that he could not pull over to the inside to let Thomas get by, with the result that he came very near to meeting his death, for the front of the Leyland looked to be almost touching his back wheel. Thomas's wonderful skill, however, saved him. He cut out at the moment when disaster was impending, and getting on the inside of Lacey he finished between the two motorcycles. Campbell won by about 300 yards and Thomas, having to slow down, was beaten for second place by a few yards by Lacey, with Knight, just behind, last – a thrilling finish, indeed. Campbell put up the fine average of 104·63 m.p.h.

*   *   *

The Boulogne Speed Trials took place this year on Thursday, 26th August. The programme started at 8.30 a.m. with a 6-kilometre run from a flying start over the undulating main road from Boulogne towards St. Omer. At 10.30 a.m., there was a hill climb over a course of 1 mile up the Baincthun hill, and then at 3 p.m. there was to be another short climb of 500 metres, both from a standing start. Finally, weather permitting, an acceleration and brake test on the Calais road was arranged for 5 p.m.

The feature of the 6-kilometre runs was the amazing performance by Segrave in the green 12-cylinder Sunbeam with which he had beaten the kilometre record at Southport some months previously. Tearing down the road which had a very indifferent surface, the car took off at the top of some of the switchbacks. Knowing that he had the Leyland-Thomas to beat, Segrave never lifted his foot, finishing with an average of 140·164 m.p.h. (1 min. 35·6 secs.). "I don't know how I ever did it," he said afterwards, "but I should never have done it had I realised my speed, and will never attempt such a thing again."

Thomas had asked Capt. Frazer-Nash, who had made an earlier run, to do what he could to see that the crowd was kept back as the Leyland tended to slew about when braking heavily after the measured run. The huge car impressed the spectators, who eagerly awaited its passage down the road. To clear the course for the racing cars, a carload of silk-armletted officials and chiefs of the gendarmerie drove down the road, calling out, "Descend into the ditch. The great cars arrive!" A quarter of an hour later, a buzzing was heard in the distance and the cry went up, "C'est Parry Thomas!". The buzzing grew louder and over the hill came a beret-clad Frenchman on a 175-c.c. motor cycle with wood-rimmed wheels and tiny cycle tyres. Thomas's run, when it did come, was fast (1 min. 55·4 secs.) and, although slower than Segrave's, secured him second place. Third fastest was R.B. Howey who had had to make a dangerous swerve at the end of his run to avoid a small motor cycle that was on the course for some inexplicable reason.

Then came the Baincthun hill climb which ended in disaster and the abandonment of the meeting.

With only their cars left on the line, Segrave and Thomas saw Howey off at the wheel of his white Ballot. He disappeared round the first bend in fine style. The third bend was a long one and here the Ballot swung broadside and, before Howey could control it, the tail caught the side of a parked car. This caused the Ballot to swing across the road, smash into a tree and roll on to its side in the ditch, a complete wreck. Howey, whose skull was fractured, had been killed instantaneously while several spectators were injured and two died. By great good fortune, Segrave was just stopped in time before making his ascent, and he and Thomas were credited with identical estimated times so that the results could be completed. The later events were cancelled.

The two Thomas Specials which were to have been driven by Thistlethwayte and Thomas in the Light Car Grand Prix on the Saturday had not been brought over after all, so Thomas made the sad journey back to England accompanying the coffin of his friend, whose car was pushed over the side in mid-Channel. *The Daily Telegraph* of 31st August 1926 contained the following paragraph:

General Sir Ivor and Lady Maxse and Mr. Parry Thomas were amongst those present at the funeral at South Ascot yesterday afternoon of Mr. Richard Barstow Howey, son of the late Major Howey, who was killed in the motor road racing at Boulogne last Thursday. Wreaths were sent by the English drivers in France, the Coldstream Guards, the Brooklands staff of the Thomas Invention Company, and the Brooklands Automobile Racing Club.

*   *   *

The B.A.R.C.'s last meeting of the year (the Brooklands Autumn Meeting) took place on 11th September and Thomas's name was down six times, to drive the Leyland-Thomas in three races and the Lanchester in three others. His first run with the Leyland-Thomas (51st 100-m.p.h. Short Handicap) was uneventful, his handicap proving too severe. His luck was still out when he competed in the 26th 90-m.p.h. Short Handicap with the Lanchester. His first win came in the 36th Lightning Short Handicap. In this event the Leyland-Thomas was behind the field for the first lap while Thomas counteracted the deficit of starting from scratch but on the second time round he passed his opponents one after another, overtaking Kaye Don, who was driving Capt. Miller's Sunbeam, in the final run down the Railway Straight to win at 115·97 m.p.h. by a mere 10 yards. Starting in the 50th 100-m.p.h. Long Handicap with the Lanchester at 11 seconds sandwiched between the Vauxhalls of J.D. Barclay (2996 c.c., scratch) and E.L. Meeson (4224 c.c., 27 secs.), Thomas got the Rapson-entered car going well but could not better the Vauxhalls which crossed the line ahead of him – first Meeson and then Barclay. This was the only placing for the Lanchester that day as its run in the 26th 90-m.p.h. Long Handicap bore no fruit.

For the final race (36th Lightning Long Handicap) Thomas was again in the Leyland-Thomas and really meant business, a fact that the bookies appeared to know when they offered "6 to 4 on". With only one non-starter (Halford's Halford Special) four other cars were competing: Campbell's 2-litre Bugatti, Barclay's Vauxhall, Barnato's Bentley and the Wolseley Viper driven by Kaye Don. On the first lap the Wolseley Viper did an unpleasant slide as it came off the Home Banking, while Thomas was busy catching up at the tail end of the race. Campbell, who had been out in front most of the time, could not compete with Thomas's third lap which was at a speed of 127·70 m.p.h. and which brought the Leyland to the front on the Members' Banking. Winning at an average of 121·20 m.p.h., Thomas had improved on his 1924 figure of 121·15 m.p.h. for the fastest average speed at which a race had been won at Brooklands.

The 200-Miles Race took place on Saturday, 25th September, and this year the Junior Car Club had devised a course with artificial corners. There was a hairpin bend at the Fork and, in the Finishing Straight itself, there were arranged two slow sandbank corners and two fast ones.

Two Thomas Specials were entered although a fortnight before the race the cars were still undergoing adjustments and alterations. The gearboxes had been modified and a change had been made to the oil circulation system. Further delay had been caused when Thistlethwayte decided to drive himself in place of Gallop, as the driving seat of his car had to be altered and this involved modifying the tanks in the tail. The work was finished in time but, on the morning of the race, a half-shaft broke and Thistlethwayte's car was a non-starter. Thomas's own car was ready but was running unsupercharged instead of supercharged as intended.

Considering the hurried preparations, Thomas must have been quite satisfied with the car's behaviour in its first race. It appeared to be a very comfortable car to drive and ran well, Thomas taking the hairpins very wide. By quarter distance, the supercharged Talbots of Divo, Segrave and Moriceau were in the lead and Thomas, somewhere in the middle of the field, had made two short pit stops, one for plugs and one for oil. Half-way through the race, Segrave led Divo and by three-quarter distance the first two positions were unaltered, but Purdy (Bugatti) had come into third place. The finishing order, which enables an assessment of the Thomas Special's performance to be made, was as follows:

1. Talbot (8 cyl. 1500 c.c.) H.O.D. Segrave   75·56 m.p.h.
2. Talbot (8 cyl. 1500 c.c.) A. Divo   74·66 m.p.h.
3. Bugatti (4 cyl. 1500 c.c.) H.W. Purdy   68·00 m.p.h.
4. Amilcar (6 cyl. 1100 c.c.) C. Martin   66·65 m.p.h.
5. Amilcar (6 cyl. 1100 c.c.) A. Duray   66·23 m.p.h.
6. Bugatti (4 cyl. 1500 c.c.) J.C. Douglas   66·21 m.p.h.
7. Amilcar (6 cyl. 1100 c.c.) A. Morel   65·62 m.p.h.
8. Thomas (8 cyl. 1500 c.c.) J.G.P. Thomas   65·37 m.p.h.
9. Salmson (4 cyl. 1100 c.c.) G. Newman   64·93 m.p.h.
10. Halford (6 cyl. 1500 c.c.) F.B. Halford   63·20 m.p.h.
11. Amilcar (4 cyl. 1100 c.c.) R. Bond   59·53 m.p.h.
12. Gwynne (4 cyl. 1100 c.c.) C.M.C. Turner   58·91 m.p.h.
13. Salmson (4 cyl. 1100 c.c.) P. Goutte   58·75 m.p.h.
14. Talbot (8 cyl. 1500 c.c.) J. Moriceau   58·60 m.p.h.
15. Austin (4 cyl. 750 c.c.) E.C.G. England   58·28 m.p.h.
16. Austin (4 cyl. 750 c.c.) G. Hendy   58·25 m.p.h.

Nobody was to know that the Brooklands meeting on Saturday, 2nd October, organised by the Essex Motor Club, was to be Thomas's last appearance at a race meeting. It is some consolation therefore to know that he had a successful day. Early in the afternoon, he drove his Leyland-Thomas in the 3-lap Essex Senior Long Handicap. Starting from scratch, both car and driver were well up to form and the blue and white colours were watched by an enthusiastic, if limited, crowd as they made their way relentlessly through the whole field to win at an average speed of

118·86 m.p.h. Second place was filled by John Cobb (Austro-Daimler) with C.M. Harvey (Alvis) third.

At the end of this race, the arrival of Prince Feisal, in his oriental robes, caused a stir in the Fork Enclosure as he made his way to the press stand to watch the racing. For his benefit, Thomas was asked to bring the Leyland-Thomas round for inspection. The Prince showed great interest and Thomas, after being introduced, saw at once that a royal request for a ride was imminent. Realising, too, that it would be impossible to say "no", and not wishing to shoulder such a heavy responsibility, Thomas's brain worked quickly and he announced that he would do a demonstration lap. Without more ado, he was in the driving seat and away. The Prince watched with approval and the crowd applauded, but one can only imagine the grin on that heavy-jowled face as the Leyland rocketed down the Railway Straight.

The meeting ended with the Essex 50-Miles Handicap for which the entries were:

	Handicap
C.M. Harvey (Alvis 1496 c.c.)	0 min. 0 sec.
G.E.T. Eyston (Bugatti 1496 c.c.)	1 min. 15 secs.
E. Poppe (Rover 2413 c.c.)	1 min. 15 secs.
J.G.P. Thomas (Thomas Special 1496 c.c.)	1 min. 15 secs.
E. Rayson (Bugatti 1996 c.c.)	1 min. 15 secs.
E. Hussey (Rolland-Pilain 1982 c.c.)	1 min. 15 secs.
H.W. Purdy (Bugatti 1496 c.c.)	1 min. 15 secs.
J. Taylor (Bugatti 1496 c.c.)	2 mins. 12 secs.
G.W. Olive (E.H.P. 1496 c.c.)	3 mins. 9 secs.
G.N. Norris (Lea-Francis 1496 c.c.)	5 mins. 3 secs.
R.F. Oats (O.M. 1991 c.c.)	6 mins. 0 secs.
G. Duller (Austin 749 c.c.)	6 mins. 19 secs.
V. Balls (Amilcar 1074 c.c.)	6 mins. 19 secs.

A. Whale (Calthorpe 1261 c.c.)	7 mins. 35 secs.
H.N. Thompson (H.N.T. 1373 c.c.)	8 mins. 13 secs.
R. Oldmeadow (Riley 1495 c.c.)	8 mins. 13 secs.
A.B. Elford (Amilcar 1074 c.c.)	9 mins. 48 secs.

A very full account of the race is to be found in *The Motor* of 5th October 1926:

With 16 starters this event proved most interesting. A.B. Elford (Amilcar) was the limit man, getting 9 mins. 48 secs. start from C.M. Harvey, who, driving the front-wheel-drive Alvis that was piloted by the Earl of Cottenham in the J.C.C. 200 Mile Race, was on scratch. On the completion of five laps, which was the period when the field began to settle down, Elford still held his lead from R.F. Oats (O.M.), G. Duller (Austin Seven), V. Balls (Amilcar) and G.N. Norris (Lea-Francis). H.N. Thompson (H.N.T. – a four-cylinder Sage-engined car with a Bugatti gearbox) retired on his third lap; G. Duller was put out of the race on his fifth lap owing to his radiator cap breaking off; and E. Hussey (Rolland-Pilain) retired before completing one lap owing to engine trouble. In the seventh circuit the leader, Elford, came in for adjustments, which, before he could resume, deprived him of his position. A lap later Oats, whose six-cylinder O.M. was running beautifully, had a useful lead, with Balls and Norris next, while J.G.P. Thomas (1500-c.c. Thomas Special), who was lapping between 107 and 108 m.p.h., had worked his way into fourth place, and was, incidentally, much faster than Harvey, whose Alvis, however, was going very well. The next retirement was E. Rayson (Bugatti), the cause being the disintegration of a tyre. Oats continued to hold his own, but it was evident that he would have to fight hard to retain his lead, for Balls, Norris and Thomas were all well in the running. One of the features of the race at this juncture was a fine duel between H.W. Purdy (four-cylinder Bugatti) and G.E.T. Eyston (eight-cylinder Bugatti) but, strange to say, Purdy's car was slightly the faster of the two. Oats's O.M. and Poppe's Rover both started to misfire and the last-named came in to change plugs and see to his undershield on the 12th lap. With Oats's engine misfiring, Balls managed to make up some ground, while Thomas did likewise, getting into third place on his 15th lap. Balls was passed by Thomas soon afterwards, and on the 18th lap Oats was caught and passed by Thomas entering the Railway Straight. Thomas eventually won by a mile from Oats at the very fine average speed of 106·19 m.p.h., his time for the distance being 29 mins. 43⅖ secs. Next came Balls, Norris and Purdy.

So, with a satisfying win in his newest car, ended Thomas's career of competitive racing. Records were still to fall to each of his three cars, "Babs", the Leyland-Thomas and the Thomas Special before the year was out, but the well-known figure in old grey flannels, Fair Isle pullover and leather helmet was to be seen no more by the "Brooklands crowd" at handicap race meetings.

A paragraph from an article in *The Autocar* gives a suggestion of what might have been the situation the following year had Thomas not been killed. It says:

First of all he has the Leyland which ran last season, then he has acquired W. Barnato's 3-litre Bentley and a 9-h.p. Riley from which great things are hoped. Besides the 1500 c.c. car which has yet more speed to come, and is something of a marvel for comfort, Thomas is constructing an 1100-c.c. straight-eight which looks well for the 200-Miles Race, and has made preparations for a special straight-eight Invicta; enough work, one would imagine, for this keen sportsman's establishment for some time to come. Added to this, Thomas has acquired the car which T. Thistlethwayte bought in preparation for last year's Grand Prix. ...

... J.E.P. Howey's Leyland will probably be converted into a touring car and will not race again.

It was in fact poor Thomas's car that was converted. After being raced in its original form by Mr. and Mrs. W.B. Scott, an advertisement in *The Autocar* shows it painted a dark colour, probably black, with headlamps, wings and two spare wheels, with the accompanying words:

LEYLAND-THOMAS No. 1

The late J.G. Parry Thomas's Famous Racing Car

Converted for touring and fitted with an attractive two-seater body by Messrs. Vanden Plas (England) 1923 Ltd. The body can be converted to a four seater by altering the position of the petrol tank.

THIS CAR HAS HELD THE WORLD'S SPEED RECORD
Full Equipment   2 Spare Wheels   6 New Tyres
SPEED – 110 M.P.H.   PRICE £675
(demonstrations given at Brooklands)

Apply: Thomson & Taylor, Brooklands Track, Byfleet, Surrey.

CHAPTER IX

Record Breaking, 1922-1926

Except for races like the 200-Miles Race and later the British Grand Prix, almost all the racing in England during the nineteen-twenties was in the form of handicap events, and it was probably for this reason as much as any other that record breaking held such a great fascination for the drivers of that period. At a time when the design of cars was developing rapidly, the potentialities of a new production could not satisfactorily be proved by racing it against machines of vastly different horsepower related only by handicaps which, cleverly devised as they were in most cases, had, of necessity, a certain degree of arbitrary guesswork about them. The test which gave definite results was the breaking of records set up by cars in the same category of engine size. As a result, a great many more attacks on existing records, or attempts to set up new ones, took place in those days than is at present the case.

It was not surprising, therefore, that, almost as soon as Thomas had arrived at Brooklands with the sports model Leyland Eight in 1922, he should want to show his car's paces in this direction. The Leyland came into Class G, which was for cars with engines not exceeding 7784 c.c., and on Thursday, 16th June, Thomas was ready on the track for his first record breaking attempt. Having made careful and accurate calculations beforehand, as he was always to do, he was undoubtedly confident of success and, at the same time, excited at the prospect. The car was weighed in at 37 cwt. 1 qr. 25 lb. and without further ado proceeded to establish the following short distance records:

Class G				Previous best	
			m.p.h.	m.p.h.	
½ mile	F/S	16 secs.	112·5	109·03	Peugeot
1 kilometre	F/S	20·04 secs.	111·62	107·6	Peugeot
1 mile	F/S	32·87 secs.	109·52	107·14	Peugeot
2 miles	F/S	1 min. 6·24 secs.	108·69	100·9	Peugeot
5 miles	F/S	2 mins. 49·98 secs.	105·89	98·87	Peugeot
10 miles	F/S	5 mins. 40·82 secs.	105·62	97·18	Peugeot

For a stripped but otherwise standard touring car, this was a very encouraging achievement and Thomas must have experienced great satisfaction from the result. It was only natural, therefore, that as soon as he had fitted the car with the pointed tail racing body, complete with undershield, and had redesigned the bonnet so that it had a blunt nose behind the standard square Leyland radiator, he should be anxious to prove its increased efficiency.

On Monday, 16th October, the Brooklands scene was again set for a further attempt, with Col. Lindsay Lloyd in charge of the official timekeeping. The Leyland was running extremely well and the records fell one after another. After 10 miles, however, the car was stopped owing to the fact that all the tyres were in a dangerous state. Thomas was using German "Continentals" which had a variegated pattern of rectangular pads in the exact centre of the tread. Under such strenuous use, it was found that the treads had parted from the canvas and Col. Lindsay Lloyd wisely forbade any further running under such circumstances. With the car showing such good form, Thomas was eager to improve on his figures but unfortunately there were no other tyres available and the attempt had to be put off. The results, this time, were:

Class G

1 mile	F/S	110·08 m.p.h.
2 miles	F/S	110·08 m.p.h.
5 miles	F/S	110·08 m.p.h.
10 miles	F/S	107·73 m.p.h.

By Thursday, 9th November, Thomas was ready to try again. The Leyland's suspension, assisted by Houdaille shock absorbers, made for good track holding and provided the driver with a comfortable ride. This time Thomas was using the, then new, Shell lubricating oil. As before, the tyres were through by the time the 10-mile record had been taken and it seems a little surprising that again there were no replacements to hand. When the results had been worked out, it was realised that the speed for 10 miles could also be claimed as a world's record, as it beat the record recently set up (113·13 m.p.h.) by Segrave on the six-cylinder Sunbeam.

Results:

Class G

½ mile	F/S	119·05 m.p.h.	
1 kilometre	F/S	118·48 m.p.h.	
1 mile	F/S	116·77 m.p.h.	
2 miles	F/S	114·91 m.p.h.	
5 miles	F/S	115·06 m.p.h.	
10 miles	F/S	114·74 m.p.h.	World's record

Within two days of the closing of the track, Count Zborowski had had a record breaking session with his 4817-c.c. Ballot and had annexed six Class records. His 116·04 m.p.h. average for 5 miles eclipsed the Leyland's figure of 115·06 m.p.h. So, with this exhilarating suggestion of rivalry, ended Thomas's first year of record breaking attempts – and a very encouraging one at that.

1923

In June the Leyland was in magnificent form and had pulled off three wins at the Essex Motor Club's Brooklands Meeting at the beginning of the month. In the last week Thomas was all set to improve his figures for the flying start records from the ½ mile up to the 10 miles in Class G. The Leyland was now fitted with Goodyear tyres and Hartford shock absorbers while its engine had a Claudel-Hobson carburetter and was running on K.L.G. plugs. Castrol oil was used this time and the petrol was Redline. To judge from the results, everything must have gone very well. Count Zborowski's 5-mile world's record was comfortably beaten.

Class G

½ mile	F/S	14·44 secs.	124·65 m.p.h.
1 kilometre	F/S	18·04 secs.	124·00 m.p.h.
1 mile	F/S	29·20 secs.	123·29 m.p.h.
2 miles	F/S	60·02 secs.	119·96 m.p.h.
5 miles	F/S	2 mins. 30·72 secs.	119·43 m.p.h. World's record
10 miles	F/S	5 mins. 9·67 secs.	116·25 m.p.h. World's record

A week later Thomas had the timekeepers out again. This time his objective was the 10-lap record (approximately 27½ miles) and the 50 kilometres. In view of his attempt the following week on the double-12-hour record, this run must have been by way of a tyre testing experiment. As well as gaining information, he pushed the records up:

Class G   *Previous best*
10 laps (S/S)   106·39 m.p.h. 105·88 m.p.h. Peugeot J. Goux
50 kilometres (S/S) 176·78 k.p.h. 170·39 k.p.h. Peugeot M. Campbell

The double-12-hour record (the use of the track at night being no longer allowed because of complaints from near-by residents) was a much coveted one owing to the magnitude of the task. The main limiting factor was, of course, the tyre problem and to this Thomas had given much thought.

The day chosen for the attempt was Wednesday, 11th July, and by then he had seen to it that a plentiful supply of tyres was available. Typical of Thomas's originality of thought, a fire-engine had been engaged to take station on the Railway Straight and to play two hoses on the track during the run-in order to provide a cooling effect on the tyres (*19*). The result was not very successful as the wet driven wheels tended to slip on the dry track and thus counteract the effect of the water. To add to Thomas's problems, the day was to prove one of the hottest in the year. Nevertheless, shortly after 6 a.m. the Leyland was away on its long run. Really thick mist made driving extremely difficult and not a little dangerous at the start, but Thomas was not to be deterred. The intention was that he should share the drive in 2-hour shifts with Capt. A.G. Miller, but this arrangement ceased abruptly during the morning when Miller was hit on the head and on the right arm by a huge section of tyre tread, rendering him momentarily insensible. In spite of his protestations, he was forbidden by the doctor who was present from any further participation.

In the first 6 hours no less than ten tyres had collapsed and it seemed certain that the reserve stock would be hopelessly inadequate. On two occasions, a tyre left the rim completely and serious delay was caused because the rivets then gave way and the flattened rim was almost detached from the disc wheel, the

Leyland having to be brought to a standstill. A car had to be despatched from the depot with a spare wheel and much time was inevitably lost.

In the afternoon, just when J.E.P. Howey, as reserve driver, was preparing to take his turn at the wheel and the signal was put out to bring the Leyland in for a refill and change of drivers, the car's differential broke and the attempt on the record had to be abandoned. Tyre trouble was the underlying cause of this failure as the extra stress on the back axle due to twice running on a bare rim at high speed was more than the differential could stand.

The main objective was unattainable but, in spite of the incessant tyre trouble, the Leyland had collected a large number of Class records during something short of ten hours running. They were as follows:

Class G		Previous best			
200 miles	93·72 m.p.h.	77·77 m.p.h.		Lanchester	S.F. Edge
300 miles	91·46 m.p.h.	81·33 m.p.h.		Lanchester	S.F. Edge
400 miles	88·05 m.p.h.	80 37 m.p.h.		Lanchester	S.F. Edge
500 miles	87·08 m.p.h.	77·43 m.p.h.		Spyker	S.F. Edge
600 miles	86·02 m.p.h.	77·10 m.p.h.		Spyker	S.F. Edge
700 miles	86·27 m.p.h.	77·10 m.p.h.		Spyker	S.F. Edge
2 hrs. 191 mi. 1610 yd.	95·96	75·48		Lanchester	S.F. Edge
3 hrs. 273 mi. 1213 yd.	91·23	75·72		Lanchester	S.F. Edge
4 hrs. 361 mi. 1422 yd.	90·45	80·28		Lanchester	S.F. Edge
5 hrs. 442 mi. 1415 yd.	88·56	80·40		Lanchester	S.F. Edge
6 hrs. 524 mi. 27 yd.	87·83	77·27		Spyker	S.F. Edge
7 hrs. 602 mi. 527 yd.	86·04	77·59		Spyker	S.F. Edge
8 hrs. 689 mi. 473 yd.	86·16	76·15		Spyker	S.F. Edge
9 hrs. 768 mi. 288 yd.	85·29	77·10		Spyker	S.F. Edge

and corresponding kilometre records.

The above virtually completed Thomas's record-breaking activities for the year. However, the last week before the closing of the track in November saw feverish activities on the part of many would-be record holders. Thomas did not bring the Leyland out again. Quite possibly he had already started on his plans for rebuilding it into its final form in which, as "Leyland-Thomas No. 1", it was to appear in 1924. He did, however, bring out the Marlborough-Thomas, fitted with a 2-litre engine and attempt, apparently without success, some of the Class B records.

J.E.P. Howey was out with his Leyland and made a number of runs in an attempt to improve on Thomas's 10 miles, Class G, record. Each run was spoiled by the ever-present tyre trouble, but finally he managed 116·41 m.p.h., which just beat Thomas, although the record could not be officially accepted until the next year.

1924

Towards the end of May, the Leyland-Thomas No. 1, which had so far only been seen in the paddock at the Easter Monday Meeting was ready to show what it could do. The new stream-lined body came in for a good deal of comment amongst the track habitués, as Thomas's idea that as little air as possible should pass between the undershield and the track was contrary to previous Brooklands practice. The car was now running on Rapson tyres, and B.P. petrol and Castrol oil were being used.

The occasion was the first attack on records in 1924 and it proved very successful indeed. The Leyland-Thomas was timed for one lap at 124·12 m.p.h. which was the fastest lap speed timed up till then; the previous fastest being 123·39 m.p.h. credited to K. Lee Guinness on the twelve-cylinder Sunbeam. From this lap, the speeds for the kilometre, mile and 2 miles were deduced. There was no attempt made on any of the longer distance records, those obtained being:

111

Class G

1 kilometre	F/S	124.12 m.p.h.	
1 mile	F/S	124·12 m.p.h.	
2 miles	F/S	124·12 m.p.h.	
5 miles	F/S	122·86 m.p.h.	World's record
10 miles	F/S	120·46 m.p.h.	World's record

Some few days after these records were taken, Thomas devoted another day (Tuesday, 27th May) to attempting the 50 kilometres and 50 miles (flying start) records. These records were held by the late Percy Lambert with his Talbot, which, it will be remembered, had been the first car to achieve 100 miles in the hour. Thomas successfully raised the 50 kilometre record from 177·76 k.p.h. to 179·31 k.p.h., automatically raising the Class G figure as well. In continuing for the 50 miles, the Leyland-Thomas's off-side front tyre burst and, in consequence, the attempt on this particular record was abandoned. What made news at the time was the fact that Thomas was using one of the newly-introduced standard pattern Brooklands silencers on the Leyland.

An excerpt from *The Autocar* (6th June 1924) serves to show that there was enthusiasm for record-breaking in France as well, although it does not seem that this particular project was ever put into practice. The two paragraphs read as follows:

Much interest has been aroused in France by the announcement that three British machines were about to be sent to the new track at Miramas, near Marseilles, with a view to lowering all world's long-distance records. Unfortunately, Mr. Lionel Rapson, who is responsible for the entire scheme, finds that he must undergo a rather serious surgical operation, and, as he is most anxious to drive during at least a portion of the time, the project has been postponed for a few weeks in order to give him time to convalesce.

The programme provides for an attempt on the old 24-hour record established by S.F. Edge in 1907, and which it ought not to be a difficult matter to lower; the establishing of a 5000-mile record, and the putting up of new records for all distances up to 50 miles. The cars to be used are J.G.P. Thomas's eight-cylinder Leyland, which would go after the short distance records, and a couple of Lanchesters for the two long-distance events. The drivers for the twenty-four hours and for the four days and four nights considered necessary to reel off 5000 miles have not definitely been appointed, but probably they will comprise, in addition to Mr. Rapson, Major Grattan and Capt. J.F. Duff. All three cars will, of course, run on Rapson tyres.

One can see now that, with a really fast car in his possession, Thomas was becoming more interested in World's records than merely Class ones. The financial gains were greater, too, and, although he was not much given to thinking in terms of hard cash, he must have realised that considerable quantities were needed to facilitate the new projects which he always had in mind.

On Thursday, 29th May, when the Wolseley Viper, driven by Capt. A.G. Miller and G.N. Norris, was attempting records in Class H, Thomas was also on the track and the Leyland-Thomas put up a world's record for 2 miles (flying start). This record, being represented by the mean of the speed in both directions, necessitated waiting for the track to be clear. In the normal, anti-clockwise, direction Thomas achieved 126·07m.p.h. and, in the reverse direction 125·96 m.p.h. – a considerable improvement on the 122·11 m.p.h. previously recorded by the twelve-cylinder Sunbeam.

The record that was so soon to become known as the "Land Speed Record" and to be competed for with great daring and at considerable expense by a number of the world's best drivers was, at this time, still quite unglamourously quoted in the list of world's records as the "flying mile" and credited to K. Lee Guinness (12-cylinder Sunbeam) at 129·17 m.p.h. It fell, without any fuss, to Thomas on Thursday, 26th June, when he again brought the Leyland-Thomas out on to the track at Brooklands. He was unable to beat the flying half-mile or the kilometre, although he bettered his own figures in Class G. His mean speed for the mile was 129·73 m.p.h. At this stage in its development Thomas had fitted a large, forward-facing tube low down on the off-side of the Leyland-Thomas's radiator cowl which connected with the carburetters and provided a form of forced induction. It may have assisted during steady speed record runs but it was soon removed, although the hole in the cowling remained (21). The day's bag of records was quite rewarding, especially the half-mile upon which Thomas had improved by nearly 10 m.p.h.

Class G

½ mile	F/S	134·33 m.p.h.	
1 kilometre	F/S	133.79 m.p.h	
1 mile	F/S	131·48 m.p.h.	(in one direction)
1 mile	F/S	129·73 m.p.h.	World's record

A week later, Thomas improved on his figure for the 5 miles (F/S) and recorded a speed of 123·81 m.p.h. for the distance, going on to push the 10-kilometres record up to 199·25 k.p.h.

On Saturday, 12th July, E.A.D. Eldridge, driving his 300-h.p. Fiat, established new world's records for the flying kilometre, the flying mile and the standing kilometre. His mean speed for the kilometre was exactly 146 m.p.h., that for the mile 145·89 m.p.h. and for the kilometre (S/S) 85·47 m.p.h. The records were run off on the road at Arpajon, near Paris, under a special permit granted by the Automobile Club of France and were the outcome of an incident the previous Sunday when Eldridge took part in the

speed trials organised by the Motocycle Club de France. To quote
The Autocar:

> In these attempts the big Fiat attained a speed of 146·8 miles
> an hour for the flying kilometre compared with 143¼ miles
> for the twelve-cylinder Delage driven by Thomas. The
> French driver, however, immediately protested against the
> Britisher's performance on the ground that the car was not
> fitted with a reverse gear, in accordance with French
> regulations. Although it was known that the existing world's
> record, set up by Lee Guinness on a Sunbeam[2], had been
> made with a car having no reverse gear, the jury, acting in
> conformity with French rules, had to disqualify the Fiat and
> give the world's record to the Delage.
>
> Eldridge immediately decided to fit a reverse and make
> another attempt on the world's records. Together with his
> assistants, he worked continuously for two days and two nights
> and was ready, at daybreak last Saturday morning, to make use
> of the national highway which had been specially reserved for
> these trials. Although having no legal right to hold up normal
> traffic, the French authorities acted in a very generous spirit by
> placing a strong force of gendarmes at the disposal of the
> organisers and in diverting all traffic from 4 to 7 a.m.

The justified but rather unsporting objection by René Thomas
goaded the other Thomas into print and this letter appeared in
The Autocar on 18th July 1924:

> With reference to E.A.D. Eldridge's very fine performance at
> Arpajon on Sunday, 6th July, in which he broke the world's
> record for the flying kilo, in such a decisive fashion (on his

---

[2] *The Autocar's* reporter appears to have overlooked Thomas's record of 129·73 m.p.h.

gigantic Fiat), only to be disqualified, according to the French papers, on an objection lodged by his opponent, René Thomas (Delage), who – again according to the French papers themselves – took advantage of an out-of-date and somewhat confused regulation, I wish to make it quite clear that I am not the Thomas who lodged the objection. The Thomas who did so is the French driver, René Thomas, who is not connected with me in any way whatever.

I should like to take this opportunity of challenging René Thomas to a match in England over 4 laps at Brooklands, and a return match over the same distance on the Arpajon track as soon as it is ready for use. My own car is a two-seater, but René Thomas is quite at liberty to use a single-seater if he prefers to, and should he prove to be the winner of either race, I shall not dig up any obsolete rules in order to have him disqualified. Surely racing drivers can still be sportsmen.

J.G.P. Thomas

Not very surprisingly, the challenge was not taken up.

Still turning over the tyre problem in his mind, Thomas decided that rain might prove a helping factor, but the following eye-witness report of his next exploit makes it clear that the idea was not a very good one. It reads:

On Monday last (21st July) J.G.P. Thomas obtained two more records at Brooklands on his straight-eight Leyland-Thomas car. These were the 100 kilometres from a standing start, covered at a speed of 175·6 k.p.h., equivalent to 109·12 m.p.h., which is a world's record, subject to confirmation, and the 50 miles class G record (for cars under 7784 c.c.) which was covered at a speed of 109·62 m.p.h. The previous figures for these two records were respectively 174·29 k.p.h., to the credit of Chassagne, on the twelve-cylinder Sunbeam, and

105·97 m.p.h. to the credit of Goux, on the Peugeot. Rapson tyres, Houdaille shock-absorbers, K.L.G. plugs, Delco ignition, Zenith carburetters, Shell spirit and Wakefield oil were used by Thomas.

This record attempt was somewhat of an experiment, as Thomas was of the opinion that a wet day would assist the tyres to keep cool, so giving them a longer life, but actually he found that the skidding which resulted from the wet track was more objectionable than the heat generated on a dry track. During most of the run rain fell heavily, and at times the car was almost invisible, owing to the water whirled up by the wheels. Several times the car skidded round to an angle of about 45 degrees, and the onlookers were much relieved when the run finished. A very bad skid on the end of the Byfleet Banking ripped off a rear tread, and later another skid resulted in the loss of a front tread also, the last few laps being done on the casing. Altogether a remarkable performance!

Thirsting for records and still more records, Thomas decided that the 6178-c.c. Lanchester which he drove for Rapson was a suitable vehicle for long distance records, and early in August he took it out on the track with remarkable success. It was fitted, naturally, with Rapson tyres and used Houdaille shock absorbers, Zenith carburetters, a Watford magneto, K.L.G. plugs, Shell petrol and Castrol oil. The results were:

Class G		Previous best		
250 kilometres	159·77 k.p.h.	156·71 k.p.h.	Sunbeam	Chassagne
300 kilometres	160·53 k.p.h.	159·77 k.p.h.	Sunbeam	Chassange
400 kilometres	157·00 k.p.h.	154·98 k.p.h.	Sunbeam	Chassange
500 kilometres	157·76 k.p.h.	154·31 k.p.h.	Sunbeam	Chassange
	2 hours	208 miles 150 yds.	104·08 m.p.h.	
	3 hours	293 miles 1272 yds.	97.91 m.p.h.	

4 hours	393 miles 651 yds.	98·34 m.p.h.
200 miles	(figure not available)	
300 miles	97·95 m.p.h.	
400 miles	98·32 m.p.h.	

* * *

An article appeared in *The Autocar* of 15th August 1924 which must have been read very carefully indeed by Thomas, for here was competition from a most unexpected quarter, and one where money appeared to be of very small consequence. Relishing, as he would, a fresh competitor and knowing exactly his own car's capabilities and ultimate limitations, the existence of the "Djelmo" may quite likely have been a deciding factor in any deliberations he may have had over the purchase of the Higham Special at the end of the year. The article ran thus:

An interesting attempt is about to be made to lower all existing short distance motor car records. In Europe the highest speed ever attained by a motor vehicle is the 146 m.p.h. for the flying kilometre established by E.A.D. Eldridge on a special 300-h.p. Fiat on the high road just south of Paris, a few weeks ago. The American sporting authorities, however, recognise the speed of 155·3 m.p.h. for the kilometre, set up by Milton on a Duesenberg, on Daytona beach, in 1920. The Eldridge record has been submitted for approval by the International Association of Recognised Automobile Clubs, but there is no European recognition of the American record, simply because there is no intercourse between the A.A.A. and European authorities.

The new car has been built in France to the special order of Mr. Djelaleddin, an Egyptian sportsman having no business connections with the motor industry, but who is intensely interested in the sport of motoring. The design of the special car was entrusted to M. Moglia, an Italian engineer, who, after being connected with motor car factories in Milan and Turin, was a member of the experimental departments of the Ballot and Talbot-Darracq companies in France.

"Djelmo" as the racing car is designated, has a straight-eight engine of 107 by 140 mm. bore and stroke, with four valves inclined in the head of each cylinder and operated by two enclosed overhead camshafts driven by a chain of spur pinions at the front. Although of unusual size, the engine possesses that purity of line for which Italian engineers are world-famous. The cylinders are in two castings of four, with their water jackets cut away and replaced by an aluminium plate to reduce weight, and are mounted very close together on an aluminium basechamber.

As all the accessory organs – water pump, oil pumps and high-tension distributors – are at the front end, the rear of the engine is free for the steering gear to be mounted on it, and the clutch and gear box form a unit bolted up to the engine basechamber. The crankshaft, which is of exceptionally big diameter, is carried in nine plain bearings; connecting rods are of I section, and the pistons are of aluminium. Lubrication is under pressure from a gear-type pump, the oil being delivered direct to the main bearings. There is a single plug per cylinder, mounted in the centre of the combustion chamber, the current being obtained from a Delco generator and delivered through a couple of distributors on the front end of each of the two camshafts.

Before being put into the chassis the engine was tried out at the French Government aeronautical laboratory at Chalais-Meudon and developed 355 h.p. at 3000 r.p.m. The test bench only being available for a limited period, the tests could not be continued, but it is reasonable to suppose that with some further tuning up the power can be increased to 400 h.p. or more. The first tests have been made with four carburetters, but changes in this direction are likely and experiments are being made with eight carburetters, each one having its own supercharger. This is a matter which will be watched with the greatest interest.

The engine is directly attached to the frame members at six points. The clutch is a multi-disc type with Ferodo fabric, and the car has one direct drive and one low gear, with a ratio of 1 to 2, in addition to a reverse. With the steering gear directly behind the cylinder block, the clutch pedal is to the left and the brake pedal to the right of the gear box. An open propeller-shaft with two universal joints transmits the power to the differential-less rear axle. Both drive and torque are taken through the semi-elliptic springs, which are under the axle and under the frame members.

When speeds of nearly 200 m.p.h. are contemplated, the greatest attention has to be paid to streamlining, and in this respect Mr Djelaleddin's car is very pleasing. The radiator is entirely enclosed by an aluminium casing forming a part of the housing over the front end of the frame members and the springs, with two wire gauze panels for the passage of air. A wind scoop carries the air over the driver's head, and the rear of the body is profiled to his body. The track is very much narrower at the rear than at the front, thus enabling the whole of the rear axle to be enclosed, while the two ends of the front axle outside the spring pads are profiled. There is no external exhaust pipe, the spent gasses being discharged through a mouth on the left-hand side of the car, just below the frame member.

Equipment of this car comprises Rudge-Whitworth wire wheels, a special type of triple Hartford shock-absorbers, and S.R.O. ball bearings throughout. The wheelbase is 9 ft. 10 ins., with a track of 56 ins. in front and 37½ ins. at the rear. Having been built in France, the car carries French colours, with the radiator housing white, the extremities of the front axle red, and the body blue.

It is quite probable that some preliminary tests will be made on the road in France within a few days, but the owner considers that in order to capture world's straightaway records it is necessary to take advantage of the most favourable natural conditions, and consequently he will send the car to America and will run it either on the dry lakes in California or on the beach at Daytona, Florida. The Californian dry lakes are preferred, for the surface does not vary to the same extent as that of the beach.

This special car has cost about 300,000 francs to build, which, at present rate of exchange, is equivalent to £3,800. Its future performance on its speed trials will be watched with interest.

*　*　*

The previous successful record attempt with the Lanchester no doubt prompted Thomas and Rapson to discuss the possibilities of an attack on the 12-hour record. With George Duller as the third driver, the Lanchester got happily into its stride at Brooklands on Tuesday, 2nd September, lapping steadily and comfortably at over 100 m.p.h. After some time, and for no very accountable reason, a spate of tyre trouble set in. The Rapson tyres, which had hitherto given good results under equally strenuous conditions, started to play up. Sixteen tyre changes had to be made, some precautionary and some because the treads had stripped. Nevertheless, and notwithstanding, the 12-hour record was achieved, the Lanchester covering 1148 miles 843 yards in the time (average 95·66 m.p.h.). This beat the world's record attained by the Sunbeam some years previously and, in addition, exceeded the world's record for 13, 14 and 15 hours as well. Nor was that all, for the car took all the Class G records from 500 to 1000 miles and from 700 to 1800 kilometres. Other than the tyre bother, the Lanchester suffered only the breakage of shock absorbers and the replacement of the magneto. Thomas, Rapson and Duller had every right to feel pleased with themselves and with their pit organisation and not least with the car.

On the same day, Dario Resta with the 2-litre Grand Prix Sunbeam achieved a standing ½ mile at over 70 m.p.h. But taking the car out again next day for official record attacks, he was killed after only three laps when his off-side rear tyre left the wheel and the Sunbeam went through the corrugated-iron fencing at the beginning of the Railway Straight, tail first, and burst into flames.

A little further light is thrown on the Lanchester's magneto trouble by a letter written by Thomas that appeared in the correspondence columns of *The Autocar*, in answer to a reader who was patriotically upholding British-made magnetos. Thomas wrote:

I regret that your correspondent "A.E.I." in *The Autocar* of 22nd August is under a misapprehension concerning the results obtained with a British magneto by me at Brooklands. The Lanchester car in question was fitted with a British magneto and also with Delco coil ignition and Exide batteries.

I regret to state that on the two occasions on which world's records have been obtained with the above car, the magneto broke down. In one case it was found necessary to run on Delco ignition only, and in the second instance the magneto was replaced with a new one and the car run on dual ignition for the rest of the trials.

J.G.P. Thomas

Pendine Sands first became the setting for a world's record when, on Thursday, 25th September, after unsuccessful attempts the day before, Malcolm Campbell achieved the world's record flying kilometre with a mean speed of 146·16 m.p.h., driving his 12-cylinder Sunbeam. When organising the Six Days Trial that year, the R.A.C. had surveyed the sands between Pendine and Laugharne and decided that they were satisfactory. Subsequently they had marked out accurate distances and produced a portable timing apparatus which was sufficiently exact. But Pendine's fame, though short lived, was to come.

By the beginning of November, the prospect of the track closing for the season produced the usual rush of record attempts, and on Tuesday, 11th November, Thomas decided to try for the 50- and 100-mile records with the Leyland-Thomas. He soon had to give up, however, as he lost a tyre as the car approached the Members' Bridge on the Home Banking and successfully, but narrowly, avoided going over the top. Two days later, he was trying again, having in the meantime drilled his team of helpers and reduced the time for a wheel change to 30 seconds. All went well for eight laps but then the Leyland was troubled by overheating and the run was spoilt. In the afternoon, with the timekeepers and officials once more in their places, the car again started to circle the track. A tyre burst after sixteen laps and, although the change of wheel was efficiently carried out, valuable time was lost. Thomas pressed on but hopes of success were not high. Towards the end of the run, the car became noticeably slower, most likely due to the same water circulation trouble, and no records were taken.

Dogged determination brought Thomas and the Leyland out again on Friday, 14th November, and this time, in spite of Thomas's dislike of Fridays, the world's hour record, which stood at 107·95 m.p.h., was the objective. Again, overheating ruined the first run and a fresh start had to be made. Lapping on the right side of 112 m.p.h., the Leyland's engine was not entirely happy for, as it turned out afterwards, there was a crack in the cylinder head. Even so, Thomas had the record well in hand and the Rapson tyres were standing up better than had been expected. His team of helpers worked wonders, even though they had to use four ordinary garage jacks, and changed all wheels in 25 seconds. After another few laps the cracked cylinder head made further running impossible and Thomas was forced to stop. Disappointment was tempered by the fact that the world's 50 miles record had been taken at 111·67 m.p.h. and also the world's 50 kilometres at 180·54 k.p.h. These were, naturally, Class G records as well.

Work on the engine over the week-end brought it back to its proper condition and on the Monday (17th November) a fresh and entirely successful attack lowered the hour record. A purely precautionary change of the Budge Whitworth wire wheels was made (about 30 seconds this time) although on closer inspection the Rapson tyres proved to be still in good condition. The world's record for 1 hour fell at 109·09 m.p.h., the car having covered 109 miles 160 yards in the time. During the same run, the records for 100 miles (108·72 m.p.h.) and 150 kilometres (174·88 k.p.h.) were taken, being both world's and Class G records.

As if that was not enough, Thomas continued to use the track on the following two days and achieved:

18th November	Class G		
200 kilometres	172·81 k.p.h.	World's record
250 kilometres	172·95 k.p.h.	World's record
150 miles	107·39 m.p.h.	World's record
19th November	Class G		
300 kilometres	166·67 k.p.h.	World's record
200 miles	103·79 m.p.h.	World's record
2 hours	104·08 m.p.h.	World's record

Brooklands track closed officially on Sunday, 23rd November, and the hard-worked Leyland-Thomas could then rest.

1925

In January, rumours were circulating concerning Malcolm Campbell and the construction of a new car in which he was installing a Napier "Lion" engine. Prince Djelaleddin's "Djelmo" had, upon completion, gone straight to Miramas for tests and tuning but no times were available as the track there was still new and rough. Early in the year, too, Thomas had purchased the Higham Special. The tempo of record breaking was un-questionably rising.

By way of clearing the decks for action to come, and as the result of a suggestion made by Col. Lindsay Lloyd on behalf of the R.A.C., the necessary arrangements were made for all Class records to be recognised on an international basis. Strict regulations were laid down to ensure accurate timing and precise measurement of distances, and the rather odd B.A.R.C. class categories were reformed so that the new international classes were, as they are today:

Class A	8001 c.c. and over.	Class F	1101 c.c. to 1500 c.c.
Class B	5001 c.c. to 8000c.c.	Class G	751 c.c. to 1100 c.c.
Class C	3001 c.c. to 5000 c.c.	Class H	501 c.c. to 750 c.c.
Class D	2001 c.c. to 3000 c.c.	Class I	351 c.c. to 500 c.c.
Class E	1501 c.c. to 2000 c.c.	Class J	up to 300 c.c.

The number of records was drastically reduced and the new internationally recognised ones were now:

1 kilometre	F/S	} mean of runs in each direction
1 mile	F/S	} mean of runs in each direction

5 kilometres	F/S	500 kilometres	S/S
5 miles	F/S	1000 kilometres	S/S
10 kilometres	F/S	1500 kilometres	S/S
10 miles	F/S	2000 kilometres	S/S
50 miles	S/S	2500 kilometres	S/S
100 miles	S/S	3000 kilometres	S/S
500 miles	S/S	3500 kilometres	S/S
1000 miles	S/S	4000 kilometres	S/S
1500 miles	S/S	1 hour	
2000 miles	S/S	3 hours	
2500 miles	S/S	6 hours	
50 kilometres	S/S	12 hours	
100 kilometres	S/S	24 hours	

* * *

The first record attempt under the new regulations was made, with a fine disregard for weather, as early as 22nd February. The intention was to attack the 24 hour record, the car was the 2-litre Grand Prix Sunbeam with which Segrave had won the race at San Sebastian the year before and which had been altered only in the matter of final drive ratio. The drivers were Major Segrave, Thomas and Count Conelli. The *venue* was Montlhéry track.

A start was called for 6 a.m. on the Sunday morning, a fact that suggested the intention of securing the 12-hour record even if weather prevented the fall of the 24. However, the night had been a cold one and the higher parts of the bankings were thickly iced. So, after Segrave had made a trial run, the attempt was postponed until the following morning.

On the Monday the car was not brought out until 8 a.m. because of the frost, but by 8.30 a.m. Segrave was in the driving seat and off. The prearranged plan was for a speed of 100 m.p.h.

to be maintained throughout the run, the car coming in each four hours for a change of driver, a change of wheels and to refuel. The weather did its worst, producing fog, bright sunshine, rain, hail and snow. Driving with great determination, Segrave kept going until 500 kilometres were accomplished and then brought the Sunbeam in. Snow had been falling gently for some time but, when Thomas took over, it started to come down in earnest. After he had been at the wheel for about half an hour, the car started to give trouble and when it had run, in all, 4 hours 35 minutes 26 seconds, it was brought in and withdrawn. Nevertheless, seven records had been broken:

International 2-litre Class   (Class E)

	m.p.h.		
50 kilometres	18 mins. 26 41/100 secs.	100·94	
50 miles	29 mins. 32 47/100	101·4	
100 kilometres	36 mins. 47 78/100 secs.	101·4	
100 miles	59 mins. 1 69/100 secs.	101·6	
500 kilometres	3 hrs. 2 mins. 28 secs.	102·159	World's record
1 hour	163·649 kilometres	101·68	
3 hours	496·064 kilometres	102·74	World's record

The Leyland-Thomas also appeared on Montlhéry track but not until early June. Without much publicity, Thomas established four new records:

Class B

5 kilometres	129·89 m.p.h.	
5 miles	129·51 m.p.h.	
10 kilometres	129·24 m.p.h.	
10 miles	122·89 m.p.h.	World's record

His next session was at Brooklands on Wednesday, 1st July, when reference is made to the fact that the Rudge Whitworth wheels were fitted with Dunlop tyres. Sharing the track with L.C.G.M. Le Champion (G.N.) and C.M. Harvey (F.W.D. Alvis), who were also attacking records, Thomas had a most successful day, as is shown by the results:

Class B

1 kilometre	S/S	76·77 m.p.h.
1 mile	S/S	88·26 m.p.h.
1 kilometre	F/S	132·99 m.p.h.
1 mile	F/S	132·30 m.p.h.
5 kilometres	F/S	124·83 m.p.h.
5 miles	F/S	124·08 m.p.h.
10 kilometres	F/S	123·56 m.p.h.
10 miles	F/S	122·31 m.p.h.

The following day, Thomas continued the good work over greater distances and lengthened the list by:

Class B

50 kilometres	113·82 m.p.h.	World's record
50 miles	114·60 m.p.h.	World's record
100 kilometres	114·63 m.p.h.	World's record

The Leyland must have been running very well and this, no doubt, spurred him on to attack one of the more coveted records about a fortnight later, when, on Tuesday, 14th July, he added the world's hour record to his bag. The new Dunlop tyres he had been using had shown their worth and, on this occasion, proved themselves invaluable. The 100 miles record went by the board at the same time.

Class B

1 hour	110 miles 1221 yards	110·64 m.p.h.	World's record
100 miles		110·47 m.p.h.	World's record

On Tuesday, 21st July, Campbell broke the world's speed record at Pendine, using, for the last time, the 12-cylinder Sunbeam. His mean speed for the kilometre was 150·869 m.p.h. and that for the mile 150·766 m.p.h. This comfortably beat the previous 145·89 m.p.h. credited to Eldridge's 300 h.p. Fiat.

Just before going over to Boulogne for the Speed Trials (1925 being the year when the Leyland-Thomas crashed during practice), Thomas took the 2-litre Thomas Special out on Brooklands and established, for the first time in the new Class "E",

1 kilometre	S/S	104·167 k.p.h. (average of runs in each direction)
1 mile	S/S	72·86 m.p.h. (average of runs in each direction)

By the beginning of September, three of Thomas's world's records had fallen to the 11-litre Delage, driven by R. Benoist who took the 5 miles F/S (133·00 m.p.h.), the 5 kilometre (221·456 k.p.h.) and the 10 kilometre (213·941 k.p.h.).

With the Leyland-Thomas in pieces, Thomas could make no further bids in this field for the rest of the year. But, by now, the Higham Special, with its huge Liberty engine, was reaching the stage when, as a Special, it was more Thomas than Higham, and Thomas's plans for it were just as complete as the car. Expressed briefly his idea was Pendine Sands with as little delay as possible.

He did, however, find time to take a fully equipped Lincoln saloon (price £1400) for an extended test on Brooklands. It was a 36-h.p. eight-cylinder model taken straight from the showrooms with a mere 400 miles on the clock. Interested, no doubt, because the car represented an American version of the type of machine he had designed himself, Thomas put it through its paces, completing a lap at 65·18 m.p.h. and registering a speed of 66·41 m.p.h. for the kilometre. Having included a run up the test hill, he spoke of the car with approval and made favourable comments on the steering and the springing.

But that was by the way. In more serious mood, he left Brooklands for Pendine Sands on 19th October to attack the record set up by Campbell's "Bluebird", "Babs" travelling down by lorry (31). For local advice on the state of the beach, Campbell had enlisted the services of Mr. Wilfred Morgan whose duties as a coastguard made him extremely knowledgeable on the subject. Thomas did not seek his advice to any great extent, respecting the feeling of loyalty that Morgan naturally felt towards the man who became known to the locals as "The Scotsman". The coastguard, nevertheless, looked upon "The Welshman" as a grand chap and gave advice when it was asked for. The weather was most unfavourable and although Thomas made several runs along the wet beach, flying spray and sand prevented any serious attempt to open the throttle. After three disappointing days at the Beach Hotel, with no sign of improvement in the elements, Thomas regretfully decided, on the evening of Wednesday, 22nd October, to load "Babs" on to her lorry and to return to Brooklands.

As a finale to 1925, "Babs" and "Bluebird" stood alongside each other at the Schoolboys' Exhibition at the Royal Horticultural Hall, while Campbell and Thomas took it in turns, on alternate days, to attend in order to answer questions and one may reasonably assume, to keep a watchful eye on the two cars.

1926

During the winter and early spring there was again talk, as there was the year before, of Prince Djelaleddin's potential record breaking 10-litre, 355-h.p. "Djelmo", which was to be driven by Foresti. Thomas was busily at work, in perhaps a more practical manner, making improvements to "Babs", some possibly suggested by the experience gained on the October visit to Pendine.

Tuesday, 27th April, saw his 27,059-c.c. car again on the Welsh sand and this time conditions were favourable. Thomas's ambitions for "Babs" were realised and she proved herself the fastest car in the world (34). After the passage of so many years one can do no better than to refer to the then current number of *The Autocar* for a description of the proceedings. It said:

As already recorded, J.G.P. Thomas averaged 169·238 m.p.h. over the flying kilometre, as a result of runs in opposite directions, and 168·074 m.p.h. over the mile in similar circumstances, on Tuesday, 27th April. Not satisfied with this, he took his car out again on the Wednesday, and raised the world's record for the kilometre to the amazing figure of 171·09 m.p.h., this, also, of course, being the average of runs in opposite directions on the course.

The full history of the series of runs which ended in such notable success is interesting. The organisation of the entire affair was in the hands of Shell-Mex, Limited, the car being transported in a Scammell six-wheeler to Pendine and back. The measured distance was indicated by a great number of flags, each stretched tightly between two posts planted in the sand, on either side of the course, making an avenue along which the car was to run. Masts supported in old oil drums buried below the surface marked the beginning and end of the measured section.

On Monday the course was marked out and tested with the aid of L.G. Callingham's well-known and sorely tried 30-98-h.p. Vauxhall, "Elizabeth-Tiger", which is a familiar feature at all race meetings, and which spent most of its time doing 70 m.p.h. *minus* its torque member. In all there were assembled ten cars, including the B.A.C. machines and signal wagon, five lorries, and seven motor cycles, six of which were used by stout-hearted policemen, in spike helmets, who ran races of their own, and the seventh by the doctor for the occasion. Fifty-three people in all were needed officially for these purposes.

A great number of large, wooden platforms, rather like rectangular duck boards, were constructed for use if "Babs" had to come to rest, in which event the wheels began to sink in the sand immediately, and a gang of men were told off and drilled to keep the car moving until it had all four wheels on the boards. The wisdom of this was shown when Lt. Com. Mackenzie-Grieve's Morris-Oxford suddenly commenced to sink with all hands and had to be dug out with much labour, thus entailing a mock court-martial later for its owner.

Thomas commenced operations on the Tuesday, when the assembly of notables from the R.A.C. had been duly penned in a roped enclosure, and the usual display of temper from the electrical timing apparatus properly overcome. "Babs" forced induction pipes over the radiator (32) had been removed, and their outlet holes in the bonnet closed up, but even then, the engine ran irregularly and emitted clouds of black smoke. There were six complete runs over the course, which, as already announced, broke both records handsomely, the best being 169·238 m.p.h. for the kilometre (272·45 k.p.h.) and 168·074 m.p.h. for the mile, while the highest speed was no less than 172·331 m.p.h. This attempt was made on 60% Shell aviation spirit and 40% benzole. Some of the other runs on ordinary red can Shell, which had been sealed and provided by the R.A.C., also broke the old world's records, but not by such a wide margin.

On Wednesday, everyone having first ascertained that Mackenzie-Grieve's car was firmly on duck boards, another run was made, the setting of "Babs" carburetters having been altered without, however, curing all the misfiring. The mean speed of the runs, nevertheless, beat the previous day's figures, and raised the average for the kilometre to the astonishing figure of 171·09 m.p.h. (275·229 k.p.h.), for the mile to 170·624 m.p.h., a truly wonderful performance, 18 m.p.h. faster than the old record. Curiously enough the best one-way run was not as good as on Monday. During all these runs the car had to be kept moving until it was safely on the boards from which it had to start, and while running Thomas had to keep up the air pressure in the petrol tank with the hand pump. Moreover, the car "snaked" considerably.

The attempt on the standing records was not successful for a curious reason. Strips of matting 30 ft. long were spread and pegged over the timing tapes, so that the car rested on one end of each strip, its front wheels nearly on the timing strip. The moment the clutch was engaged the Dunlop-tyred wheels raced madly, creating such intense heat that the water came away from them as steam and the smell of burning rubber was intense, the car slewed sideways off the mats, and the time thus lost at the start frustrated the attempt entirely. Moreover, "Babs" began to sulk a little and the misfiring became worse. During this day's run the mixture of aviation spirit with benzole was again used. Shell triple oil was in the engine throughout.

Several Brooklands enthusiasts were present, R.B. Howey and J. Cobb from the start, J.E.P. Howey driving up from Selsey one day, then returning home the same day. Obviously, Thomas can do even better, and a maximum of

200 m.p.h. is not so very unlikely at some future date in more favourable circumstances.

The equipment of the car included, besides the items already mentioned, K.L.G. plugs, Float-on-air cushions, Coventry chains, four Zenith carburetters, Hartford shock absorbers, an Auster-Triplex screen, Marles steering, Terry valve springs, Rudge-Whitworth wheels, Delco ignition with C.A.V. battery, Laystall camshafts, Ferodo brake linings, Miralite pistons, Tecalemit lubrication, and Wellworthy piston rings. The engine had been practically redesigned and rebuilt by Thomas and the chassis completely altered.

In recognition of his competitor's achievement. Campbell most sportingly wrote:

I should like to add my heartiest congratulations to the many others which Mr. J.G. Parry Thomas has received after his recent attack on world's records.

To break old world's records with a margin of over 20 m.p.h. is a truly marvellous performance, deserving of the highest praise, and one which will never be forgotten. Whether these records stand or not matters little, as Mr. Thomas will always have the satisfaction of having been the first man in recent years to have beaten the most coveted records by this huge margin.

Malcolm Campbell

Prince Djelaleddin, over in Paris, admitted freely that Thomas had accomplished a wonderful sporting performance. "However, I think that 'Djelmo' is sufficiently more modern," he is quoted as saying, "to be able to beat 'Babs', and, in any case, there will be some good sport during the next few weeks."

Transport problems caused by the General Strike postponed the arrival of the "Djelmo" in England. They also provided Thomas with several days of lighthearted amusement driving a London bus. A number of apocryphal stories are told concerning his exploits as a bus driver but the all-over impression one gets is that not all the stopping places were respected as this would have "spoilt his time". The flavour, at any rate, is most certainly Thomas-like.

To finish the story of the "Djelmo", which never ran on Pendine until after Thomas's death, it may be said that the money spent on the car was not justified by the results. After weeks of tuning in the garage at the Beach Hotel, Pendine, and of trials on the beach when side winds would lift the wheels of the over-light, crab-tracked car, Foresti made a bid for the record and the car overturned, throwing out its driver after one revolution during which the sand removed all the hair from the top of his head. Foresti, an extremely tough little man, walked away from the wreck but subsequently collapsed and was taken to hospital in Carmarthen to recover.

* * *

The rebuilt Leyland-Thomas, which had first appeared at the Easter Meeting at Brooklands, was out after records again on Tuesday, 8th June. Although it was, practically speaking, a new car, it kept up the victorious tradition of its older self, breaking a world's record and two Class B ones, thus:

Class B

5 miles	126·35 m.p.h.	
10 kilometres	126·26 m.p.h.	
10 miles	126·03 m.p.h.	World's record

A week later (15th July) Thomas carried the process a little further and established new Class B records for the standing kilometre and the standing mile.

1 kilometre	S/S	124·48 k.p.h	77·35 m.p.h.
1 mile	S/S	88·47 m.p.h.	

During the summer his time was taken up with race meetings and the final stages in the evolution of the 1½-litre "flat iron" Thomas Special. However, as soon as the racing season was over, Thomas's thoughts were back on records. He decided that he would try, with the Leyland-Thomas, for as many records as could be taken in 8 hours and, with this end in view, he trained his band of willing helpers to a high degree of efficiency in the changing of wheels and tyres. On Thursday, 7th October, all was set and he started away in the Leyland at 8.20 a.m. All went well for 24 laps. Then he lost the tread from his offside front tyre. After a quick wheel change, he continued until his first scheduled stop at 64 laps The intended 15 seconds for fuel, oil and change of wheels was extended to nearly double that time because the semi-rotary hand pump for refuelling proved a serious and handicapping mistake. Some twenty minutes later, another tyre went and the Leyland-Thomas was in again. The second scheduled refuelling stop was followed by further tyre trouble and at the end of some six hours driving Thomas came in. He was too tired and dazed to make it safe to continue. George Duller, who was to co-drive, had been delayed and had not arrived. M. Paul Dutoit, who was there, gallantly offered to fill the gap. Knowing little about the car, Dutoit made a fine effort, lapping around 100 m.p.h. Having had time to think, Thomas decided that too much time had been lost through slow refuelling and tyre troubles and that it was not right to let Dutoit go on. He was called in and the attempt ended. Three world's records had been taken and as Thomas said, "That's not so bad."

Class B

500 kilometres	179·027 k.p.h.	World's record
1000 kilometres	176·655 k.p.h.	
500 miles	110·04 m.p.h.	World's record
3 hours	111·28 m.p.h.	333 miles 1477 yds. World's record
6 hours	109·96 m.p.h.	659 miles 1317 yds.

With the track due to close for repairs on 1st November, time was growing short, but Thomas still had plans for more record breaking. "Babs's" turn for a run came on Thursday, 14th October. With her 27 litres, there was no doubt about her qualifying for Class A (8000 c.c. and over) but at the same time the track at Brooklands was not at all suited to her particular capabilities. However, as was his habit, Thomas had made careful calculations beforehand and was quite confident that he could achieve the results he intended. He was seldom wrong and, at the end of the day, the following records had been set up:

Class A		*Previous best*	
5 miles	124·25 m.p.h.	116·75 m.p.h.	Sunbeam
10 miles	122·91 m.p.h.	121·42 m.p.h.	Fiat
10 kilometres	123·91 m.p.h.	not previously set up	

While the Land Speed Record naturally held pride of place in the imagination of the public, amongst racing men the "Hour" has always been an historical and much coveted record. It had recently been taken by Ortmans' Panhard, but Thomas felt that it was still within reach of the Leyland-Thomas which had, of course, held it twice before. Knowing, as one now does, that this occasion, on Thursday, 21st October, was to be Thomas's last drive in this famous and successful car of his, it is most gratifying that the second run should have been such a complete success.

The first run, in the morning, was spoilt by the Leyland cutting out on two cylinders during the last five laps. When Thomas came in, Col. Lindsay Lloyd was unable to say at once whether the record had fallen or not. After a thorough check, it appeared that it had been missed by 253 yards. Thomas's comment was typical. "Right," he said, "I'll have another try later in the day, if I may. I don't think there is anything so wrong with the car that I can't deal with on the spot."

In spite of the Leyland's weight and speed, the Dunlop tyres stood up remarkably well. For the hour record they were indeed a vital factor, as a burst would undoubtedly have put paid to the attempt. At the end of his second and successful run it was obvious that they had made it, but only just, as one tyre was in no state to continue. The Leyland-Thomas had this time achieved 121 miles 1307 yards, averaging 121·74 m.p.h. At the end of the day, Thomas drove the car up to Selfridges where it was put on view to the public during the following week.

At this point, a look at the list of holders of the hour record is of interest.

World's Hour Record

1907	S.F. Edge	Napier	70 miles 130 yards
1907	Clifford Earp	Thames	76 miles 453 yards
1908	F. Newton	Napier	85 miles 555 yards
1909	C. Smith	Thames	89 miles 892 yards
1912	L. Coatalen	Sunbeam	92 miles 915 yards
1912	V. Hemery	Lorraine-Dietrich	97 miles 1037 yards
1913	P. Lambert	Talbot	03 miles 1470 yards

1913	J. Goux	Peugeot	106 miles 387 yards
1913	J. Chassange	Sunbeam	107 miles 1672 yards
1924	J.G.P. Thomas	Leyland	109 miles 160 yards
1925	J.G.P. Thomas	Leyland	110 miles 122 yards
1926	M. Ortmans	Panhard	116 miles 150 yards
1926	M. Ortmans	Panhard	120 miles 422 yards
1926	J.G.P. Thomas	Leyland	121 miles 1307 yards

*   *   *

On the last day before the track closed, Saturday, 30th October, Thomas brought off another *coup*. This time it was the 1500-c.c. Hour record, and at 11 o'clock he drove up to the starting line in the 1½-litre straight-eight Thomas Special which was now running for the first time in its complete form, as designed with supercharger. Thomas adjusted his goggles and waited for the signal from Col. Lindsay Lloyd. Once away, the car ran magnificently and streaked round for lap after lap without a falter. The record fell at the first attempt, two other records being collected en route, and Thomas finished fresh and cheerful, remarking that, compared to the Leyland-Thomas, the control of the "flat iron" was a two-finger job.

The previous best performance had been put up by E.A.D. Eldridge (Eldridge Special) at Montlhéry, when he covered 107 miles 1094 yards. Thomas's figures were:

International Class F

100 kilometres	33 mins. 23·09 secs.	111·67 m.p.h.
100 miles	53 mins. 17·09 secs.	112·60 m.p.h.
1 hour	112 miles 1363 yards	112·77 m.p.h.

The car's equipment was as follows:

Fuel: Shell Aviation and benzole mixed.
Oil: Triple Shell.

K.L.G. plugs, Dunlop tyres, Rudge Whitworth wheels, Solex carburetter, Marelli magneto, Hartford shock absorbers, Ferodo clutch and brake linings.

The steel used throughout in the construction of the car was Kayser-Ellison. Ball bearings were Ransome and Marles and the crankshaft and big-ends were lined with Hoyt metal.

The track now closed and Thomas could take his ease, if such it could be called, with pencil, paper and the slide-rule which, according to report, he "manipulated like a pack of cards", and work out the final details of his next attack on the Land Speed Record.

That he had other irons in the fire is evident from a paragraph which appeared in *The Motor* on 2nd November 1926. It said:

Mr. J.G. Parry Thomas and Mr. N.T. Chamberlayne have entered into business together as selling agents for any type of car, trading as Parry Thomas and Chamberlayne at 220 Great Portland Street, London, W.I. Mr. Thomas's staff of mechanics at his works at Brooklands track is available for any complete overhauls.

The Leyland-Thomas and the Thomas Special were proudly displayed in the Great Portland Street showroom window during the winter and presumably a certain amount of business was done. However, after Thomas's death the following March, it became evident that Mr. Thomson and Mr. Taylor did not see eye to eye with Mr. Chamberlayne. As a result, Mr. Chamberlayne was bought out and the remarkable and successful firm of Thomson and Taylor came into being.

Leylands had not forgotten their ex-chief Engineer for on Thursday, 9th December, in their decorated canteen, Thomas found himself among 300 employees of the firm attending a supper and concert party as a guest of the directors. He made a light-hearted speech in reply to his welcome and included his congratulations to three other stout-hearted record-breakers present, albeit in a different category from his own, who had just completed a journey from Singapore to London in a Trojan car.

CHAPTER X

Disaster, 1927

E.A.D. Eldridge might be said to have anticipated 1927 by starting to break records on New Year's Eve. Driving a 2-litre Miller on the Montlhéry track, he broke three world's records – the 100 kilometres and the 100 miles, which were previously held by Ortmans (Panhard-Levassor), and the hour record which Thomas had acquired in October at 121·74 m.p.h. The Miller's figures were:

100 kilometres	126·8 m.p.h.
100 miles	127·1 m.p.h.
1 hour	126·51 m.p.h.

Also, during the last days of the old year, Campbell took his new Napier-Campbell down to Pendine. The car, which weighed over 3 tons ("Babs'" weight was only 35 cwt.) was completely untried. It had most purposeful and attractive lines, not at all unlike an overgrown Bugatti. Thomas was naturally immensely interested and was down at Pendine on 2nd January when the new "Bluebird" was run down the ramp on to the beach. A trial run showed at once that all was not well with the gearbox and for some time, with the car on boards because of its tendency to sink into the sand, Thomas and Campbell discussed what should be done. Campbell's mechanics worked all night on the gearbox and next day he tried again, but top gear would still not engage properly. It became evident that nothing more could be done on the spot and so the car was taken back to Campbell's workshop at Povey Cross.

Trying again on Saturday, 22nd January, luck was still against the "Bluebird". The beach was in a waterlogged condition, but the course was marked out and Campbell was determined to see what his machine could do. In one direction, he achieved 172·869 m.p.h. over the mile and, according to his rev. counter, attained 176 m.p.h. for a short distance. The record, however, stayed where it was. Neap tides prevented further record attempts before February and so "Bluebird" was taken back home again.

Thomas was quietly confident that "Babs" was capable of going a good deal faster. Considerable work had been done on the car since the year before. Improvements had been made to the induction system and a new radiator, sloping more sharply backward than the old one, had been fitted, reducing the bluntness of the nose (26). The whole car had been lowered and a light aluminium fairing now covered the chains. Brooklands track was still undergoing repairs, but Thomas had managed to use about a mile of it for test purposes, though with "Babs" it must have seemed maddeningly short.

Events were now moving very fast indeed. Sunbeams had produced a huge two-engined 1000-h.p. car for Segrave to drive and, now that America had become a member of the International Association of Recognised Automobile Clubs, world's records on the other side of the Atlantic would be recognised. Segrave was therefore going to Florida where the Sunbeam would have ample space.

Then, on Friday, 4th February, the news came that Campbell had set up a new speed record with the Napier-Campbell on Pendine Sands. Like Thomas, he was eager to be the first man to record 180 m.p.h. but this had not been possible. From the

Pendine end of the beach, his first outward run was at 179·158 m.p.h. but on the return run his goggles were shaken off when the car hit a bump and Campbell was nearly blinded by sand and spray. The mean figure was a record all the same: 174·883 m.p.h. over the kilometre and 174·223 m.p.h. over the mile. In the hopes of bettering this time, Campbell made two more runs but they were not so good as the first ones.

Thomas had booked accommodation at the Beach Hotel for 14th February, but he was prevented, by an attack of influenza, from keeping to this date. Knowing full well that Campbell intended to make a further bid as soon as he could and that Segrave was due to leave England on 1st March in the "Berengaria", Thomas arranged to be at Pendine on 1st, 2nd and 3rd March.

When the time came, he was not fully recovered from his 'flu but he drove down to Pendine just the same, feeling all the better for the fresh air on the run. "Babs" travelled down on a tarpaulin-covered trailer behind a lorry. Arrived at the Beach Hotel, Thomas found that conditions were far from ideal. On the Tuesday, he was on and off the beach watching for a break in the weather. He was looking older than his 41 years and the effect of his recent illness was not helped by the old leather coat and the battered trilby hat that he wore.

Throughout the next day the weather was still poor, and Thomas continued to wait for an improvement, spending some of the time in bed. Commander Mackenzie-Grieve was in charge of operations and Major Callingham was there as Thomas's technical adviser. Col. Lindsay Lloyd was in control of the time-keeping arrangements on behalf of the R.A.C. while Mr. Buckley represented Dunlop's and Mr. Delacour, Shell.

Thursday (3rd March) was more promising and Thomas, who had broken so many records on that day of the week, decided to make his bid. "Babs" was run down the slipway from the road by the hotel (35) and the officials took up their posts. As arranged, Major Callingham waited until Thomas was ready to start and then drove down the course in his 4½-litre Bentley to warn the timekeepers that "Babs" was to be expected. On the first run out and back, Thomas travelled fast but not fast enough, "Babs" making a considerable amount of black smoke. The car was then turned, slight alterations were made to the carburetter settings and the plugs were changed. On receiving the signal from Thomas that he was ready again, Major Callingham, with Thomas's mechanic, Jock Pullen, beside him in the Bentley, tore down the beach, keeping well over to one side of the course. Before he was clear of the measured mile, "Babs" flew past him in a cloud of spray, sand and exhaust. The Bentley eased up but as the haze cleared, Major Callingham saw flames and ominous black smoke. Opening the throttle again, the Bentley rushed on down the beach to be met with the most horrifying sight. "Babs" had swung round and was facing out to sea. Her near-side front wheel was at a drunken angle while her off-side rear one had ceased to exist, and her engine was on fire (36). Poor Thomas, the top of his head completely taken off by the whip of the broken driving chain, was lying half in and half out of the car. Pullen bravely lifted the body from the blazing machine, getting burnt in the process, and laid it on the sand.

The sad news travelled like wildfire, and a heavy gloom fell over Pendine. After some time, a motor tender drove slowly down the beach, taking Thomas's remains to rest in the garage which had been occupied by his beloved "Babs". The wrecked car itself was taken in tow by a tractor and deposited just below the sea front; it being impossible to haul it up on to the road that night.

At the inquest the following day, Major Callingham explained how he thought the accident had happened. The off-side driving chain had broken and must have struck Thomas on the head,

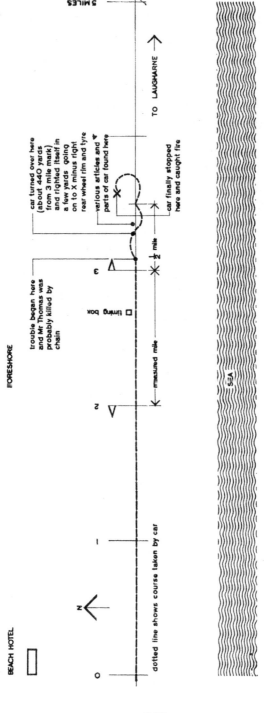

Figure 6. Diagram Diagram of "Babs" last run, re-drawn from a plan by Major L.G. Callingham for the inquest

killing him instantly. The rear wheel was torn off, causing the tail to tip up into the air. This displaced the front wheel and the car slithered upside down for some distance, then righted itself and continued in its original direction for three or four hundred yards, finally making a left-handed circle and coming to rest facing the sea (37).

The inquest was presided over by Dr. R.L. Thomas, the coroner for West Carmarthenshire, and the verdict was pronounced that "Mr. Thomas had died from wounds in the head which were the result of a motor accident."

No one will ever know exactly what happened. There are those who consider that Thomas lifted his foot at the end of the measured mile before declutching, causing the chain to ride up on the driving sprocket and break. Others are of the opinion that a front tyre burst overturning the car, travelling as it was at very high speed, and that its driver was decapitated when the machine turned over, but the photograph of the wrecked car seems to refute this possibility. These views, however, are not very convincing when contrasted with the theory that was deduced on the spot by Mr. Reid Railton.

Knowing that Thomas was going to attempt the record that afternoon, Railton drove over to Pendine, arriving at about 3 p.m. He at once heard that his friend had been killed some half an hour earlier. Being naturally very concerned and upset, he was, at the same time, determined to find out the cause of the accident. Having no official position, he was free to spend as long as he needed to examine the car, and after careful inspection of each tooth of the driving wheel sprocket, he found one in which there was an indentation. This dent could only have been made by something harder than the steel of which the sprocket was made. The only harder steel used was that of the wheel spokes and, trying a piece of broken spoke in the dent, he found that it fitted. Building his theory from this, Railton decided that the off-side rear wheel had collapsed at speed, it being a well-known fact that wire wheels do not stand up well to the snatch of chain-drive, and that a piece of spoke had lodged between the chain and the chain-wheel breaking the chain as a result. With full power on the driving sprocket, the free length of chain would fly upwards, while the car would, at the same time, heel over in the direction of the collapsed wheel flinging Thomas towards the flying chain. After that, with no one controlling her, "Babs" ran amok.

After the inquest was over, an idea for towing the car out to sea was abandoned and it was decided to bury it in the sand dunes. The first hole was made too near the beach and it filled with water, but a second, further inland and on property then belonging to two brothers named Johns, was dug to the depth of six or seven feet. A farm tractor towed the wrecked machine to the edge of the grave and before pushing it in, every part, including the cylinder block, was smashed. To discourage the possibility of souvenir hunting, even Thomas's leather coat was slit to pieces before it was thrown in, in company with the macabre driving helmet.

In spite of rumours to the contrary, there was never any attempt made to dig the car up in later years, and now that the land is owned by the Ministry of Supply as part of an experimental rocket range, "Babs" will never be disturbed. For over the very spot stands the police office adjacent to the western entrance.

Thomas's body was taken back to Weybridge, although floral tributes arrived at the Beach Hotel, including a huge model of a car made in violets, bearing a card with no name but only the words, "Ride on, ride on, in majesty."

The following Monday afternoon (7th March) his body was taken to "The Hermitage", inside the track, where a private service was attended by his mother, Mr. and Mrs. Gordon Jones and Mr. and Mrs. Whiffen (his sisters and brothers-in-law), Mr. Kenneth Thomson, Mr. and Mrs. Duke-Williams (his housekeeper and her husband) and Mr. K. Taylor. After the service, the coffin was taken through the paddock to Byfleet Church. Besides the wreaths on the hearse, six other vehicles were required to carry the remainder. Some of the flowers came from:

Mrs. Thomas
Mr. & Mrs. Gordon Jones
Mr. & Mrs. Harold Whiffen
Mr. & Mrs. Whiffen, senior
Marcus, Phillip and Hardy Whiffen
Kenneth J. Thomson
Anne and Mr. and Mrs. Duke-Williams
Mr. and Mrs. K. Taylor
Mr. & Mrs. S.T. Saunders
All his employees at Brooklands
Staff at Spring Gardens
The Hon. David Tennent
Mr. Wren
Dame Ethel Locke-King
Col. & Mrs. Lindsay Lloyd
B.A.R.C. Staff
B.A.R.C.
R.A.C.
Sir Charles Wakefield, C.B. and Mrs. Nixon
Henry Spurrier, senior
Henry Spurrier, junior
Chairman & Directors of Leyland Motors
General Manager & Staff of Leyland Motors
The Old Workmen who knew him at Leylands
R. Railton
Les Coureurs Automobiles de France
Le Commission Sportif of the Automobile Club du Nord de la France, Boulogne-sur-mer

Neville Tankerville Chamberlayne
Pat Morgan
The Staff of Parry Thomas and Chamberlayne
John Cobb
Richard Ward
Commander Mackenzie-Grieve
Leslie Callingham and Delacour
Dunlop Tyre Fitters
Raynes Park Lodge of Freemasons No. 4377
Junior Car Club
Essex Motor Club
Surbiton Motor Club
Race Drivers' Club
The Motor and The Light Car & Cyclecar
Shell-Mex Ltd.
Directors of K.L.G.
Dunlop Rubber Co. Ltd.
T.B. André & Co. Ltd.
Laystall Engineering Works Ltd
Sunbeam Motor Co. Ltd.
Rudge-Whitworth & Co. Ltd.
Wellworthy Ltd.
Peter Hooker Ltd.
Zenith Carburetters Ltd.
Bentley Motors Ltd.
Salmson Motors Ltd.
Invicta Cars
Quadrant Tradesmen at Weybridge
Capt. Malcolm Campbell, and Staff
Lanchester Motor Co. Ltd.
Mr. and Mrs. George Duller
Dr. Dudley Benjafield
E. Lanzerotti-Spina

Rosemary Binks
Ursula Whalley
All at Beach Hotel, Pendine
Jack Howey
Dick Howey's Sisters
Mrs. Francis Howey
Allan Hess
Woolf Barnato
June
Mr. P.L. Rapson
K. Lee Guinness
G.E.T. Eyston
Eustace Moyes and Dudley Watt
Mr. Charles West
Mrs. Norman Norris and Miss Annie Houghton
Dr. Eric Gardner
Capt. & Mrs. Crosby Meakes
Scottle
Mr. & Mrs. Crook
Mrs. and Miss Hope
Mr. Alfred Ellison
Doreen Horn
Mrs. Falcon Stuart
Capt. & Mrs. Malcolm Campbell
Miss Violet Cordery
Capt. & Mrs. Macklin
Nada, Lance and Mia
Phil Turner
Mrs. F.T. Harris (Long Tom's widow)
Cyril and Mrs. Durlacher
Dennis, Kenneth and Doreen Evans
C.F. Temple
P.V. Field

W.O. Kennington
Ken and Vera
Mr. Motley
Little Joan
Valerie
Dido
Miss Addis Price
Jack Crickmay
Rosemary
John Pugh
Reginald Spring
Mrs. Rice
Mr. and Mrs. McCormack
Mr. Buckley
Ivy Cummings
George Newman
Sir Roland and Lady Gunter

There was a very large gathering at Byfleet Church and, after the Service, Thomas was laid to rest in the churchyard, his goggles being buried with him.

A granite stone with a large black cross stands at the head of the grave bearing the words:

JOHN GODFREY PARRY THOMAS
BORN 6TH APRIL 1885

ACCIDENTALLY KILLED ON PENDINE SANDS
WHEN ATTEMPTING WORLD'S MOTOR SPEED RECORD
3RD MARCH 1927
Life is eternal and love is immortal
and death which is only the horizon
is nothing save the limit of our sight.

Postscript

A clear picture of what happened to Thomas's cars after his death would make a satisfactory epilogue to the story of his life. The passage of time and the intervention of the Second World War, however, have clouded the issue to such an extent that it is doubtful whether a complete and detailed record can ever be pieced together. Nevertheless, it is possible to give some details.

The Leyland-Thomas No. 1 which had served Thomas so well and faithfully first passed into the hands of Mr. and Mrs. W.B. Scott. It was repainted black and green and was run at Brooklands for the next year or two, being sometimes driven for Mrs. Scott by John Cobb. It was then fitted with a two-seater touring body by Vanden Plas, as already mentioned in a previous chapter, and was offered for sale by Thomson & Taylor's. It appears next in the ownership of R.J. Munday, who altered the body slightly, giving it a long-tailed shape once again. With a small racing windscreen and with the wings removed, he used the car in competition until the Whitsun Meeting of 1936 when the engine blew up, the undershield and crankcase falling on to the track and the car catching fire. Munday removed the car to his yard in the Battersea Bridge Road intending to restore it at some future date, but it was still there when the war started and was completely destroyed during an air-raid later on.

Howey's Leyland-Thomas, which, at the end of the 1926 season, was reported to be going to have a touring body fitted, got as far as the workshops of Blythe Bros, of Canterbury, who had carried out bodybuilding for Count Zborowski, where it was given a fabric coupé body and fitted with front wheel brakes. It appears to have been rescued in the nick of time by Dudley Froy, who bought it and gave it a new lease of life by fitting the chassis with the body shell from the Leyland-Thomas No. 1 and retaining the front wheel brakes. The engine size was now quoted as 95 by 140 mm. (8468 c.c.). The original Thomas colours of pale blue and white were altered and for the rest of its existence the ex-Howey Leyland had a cream-coloured body with the chassis painted dark brown.

In 1932 Mr. and Mrs. T. Wisdom were on the look-out for a suitably powerful car with which Mrs. Wisdom might challenge the unofficial Ladies' Lap Record at Brooklands, then held by Mrs. Scott. The Leyland was for sale, they bought it, and the Ladies' Lap Record fell to Mrs. Wisdom at 121·47 m.p.h. in September of the same year. Looking back on those days, she said recently that she found the car easy to handle, even modestly suggesting that the Leyland practically drove itself. Those who have witnessed Mrs. Wisdom's skill at the wheel, however, will make a mental note that the slightly-built driver, wedged into the seat by a large cushion, was undoubtedly of considerable assistance to the Leyland-Thomas as it lapped at over 120 m.p.h. She did recall that the car always tended to snake as it came on to the Home Banking but she went on to explain that there was no harm in letting it do that if it wanted to. After breaking the Ladies' record, the car was penalised by stiffer handicaps and the Wisdoms did not have much further success with it. They sold it in 1934. Its subsequent history fades until its last hour, during the war, when it was reduced to scrap metal in a breaker's yard in Eastbourne.

The Marlborough-Thomas cars have disappeared without trace, though it seems more than probable that these cars were converted and improved into the two 4-cylindered Thomas Specials that followed. All that is known of these cars is that one was bought by Felix Scriven, who converted it into a Scriven Special. There is, in fact, a Scriven Special still in existence today, but although it uses a Hooker-Thomas engine, its appearance does not in any way suggest that of a Thomas Special.

More is known about the two 1½-litre "flat-iron" straight-eight Thomas Specials but, again, time has obscured the complete picture. One of these cars was purchased by H.W. Purdy and the other by W.B. Scott. Both cars were entered for the 1927 200-Mile Race, Purdy achieving 5th place in the general order and 2nd place in the 1500-c.c. class. The second car was a non-starter as, at the last moment, Scott elected to drive a Bugatti instead. In the R.A.C. Grand Prix of the same year the two cars were running again (Purdy's blown and Scott's unblown) but they each retired before full distance. In the 1928 200-Mile Race, Purdy again was a starter but this time he was shunted by another car during the first lap and crashed into the railings at the approach to the Fork, bending the Thomas Special's chassis. The car was repaired and Purdy raced it at Brooklands meetings up to the end of 1931.

In the following year the car became the property of R.J. Munday and remained in his possession until after 1935, in which year he had removed the Thomas engine and fitted a 2·7-litre Perkins diesel. With the car in this form he established records for diesel-engined cars including the flying start kilometre at 94·7 m.p.h. In order to accommodate the Perkins engine, the flat top of the bonnet now had a somewhat camel-like hump. After Munday had disposed of it the car passed through the hands of a number of owners and various engines were fitted to it. The body and chassis now belong to Mr. Ian Clark, of Hampstead, who showed the car, minus an engine, as an exhibit at the Brooklands Golden

Jubilee. He hopes to be able to restore the car eventually to its original condition if one of the straight-eight engines can be found. He also possesses the blueprints of the chassis of the 750-c.c. car which was never completely constructed.

The second and unsupercharged Thomas Special purchased, as already mentioned, by W.B. Scott, passed on to E.M. Thomas (no relation to its designer) and then has become lost. Sometime in 1936 a Thomas Special was known to be in the possession of a metal merchant in North London by the name of Bradley and this was in all probability the same car. Rumour has it that a Thomas Special is now in America and is fitted with a Mercury V.8 engine, and this may be the same car again, but no doubt it is getting far from the original Special that Parry Thomas built.

It appears that three engines of the 1½-litre straight-eight type were made and it is known that one blew up while on the test bench.

The history and present whereabouts of the hypothetical 750-c.c. car is all but unknown. The chassis parts are reported to have been seen and these included a spare front axle still in its wrappings. Some work on this car was undoubtedly done during Thomas's lifetime but, as has already been stated, the intended engine was never made and so from the point of view of association with Thomas's activities this shell, wherever it may be, is not of very great interest.

The white Leyland-Thomas two-seater, so beautifully restored in recent years by Leyland Motors Ltd, is now on loan to the Montagu Motor Museum at Beaulieu. Although Thomas was not responsible for its construction, as it was assembled after his death, it is none the less a fine and impressive piece of machinery and it is to be hoped that those who now pause to look at this magnificent motor car will think for a moment of John Godfrey Parry Thomas, that quiet genius and much loved sportsman whose end was so tragic.

Appendix A

The following article appeared in The Light Car and Cyclecar *(which has now ceased publication) for 27th December 1926, and is reproduced by kind permission of The Temple Press Ltd.*

THE CHALLENGE FROM AMERICA
The present situation in the world of racing discussed by
J.G. Parry Thomas

A new atmosphere in the motor sporting world has been created by the admission of America into the international circle, and an entire readjustment of ideas as to world's records has to be made. For a number of years America has been building a castle, and the signing of the agreement at the recent meeting of the International Association of Recognised Clubs enabled her to take possession; in other words, certain records have been established in America, but until the meeting referred to, they did not bear the all-important stamp of international recognition.

We can still claim to have built the fastest cars in the world, but we have to face the fact that America can, and has, beaten many of our figures, both for short and long distances, and we have to inquire into the possibility of that country sweeping the board in forthcoming record-breaking attempts and international races; but wait a moment.

American supremacy – so far as it goes – is due primarily to the fact that the monetary resources at the command of her pioneers in motor racing are immense, and in a secondary degree to the wonderful board tracks which she possesses.

The former results in a machine which, by no means superior to our own in design, has the advantage of being constructed of the very finest materials the world of engineering can produce; moreover, experimental work, one of the most costly items in the perfection of a racing car, continues unhampered.

If this were not enough the prize money offered in connection with the larger events is well worth striving for, thus providing a practical incentive to the drivers themselves.

Now, when these perfect cars are launched on perfect tracks, every driver intent on covering himself with honour and glory and, incidentally, of reaping the practical reward of his skill and daring, is it to be wondered at that the speeds of American cars are higher on the average than ours?

We are not so wealthy a country when it comes to footing the bill for racing ventures; in fact, there have been quite a number of "one-man" shows. We are handicapped at the outset; but we *can* take the war into the enemy's country by attempting records over the ground that favours our protagonists so markedly. Further, we have yet to see what American cars can do in international events and over courses in Europe in the selection of which she has no choice. Then surely our cars, built to withstand rougher conditions, ought to shine; surely there will be a levelling out, a far more practical datum line upon which to base the struggle for future records and racing successes?

We must assimilate all this thoroughly; we must bear in mind that until we can meet Americans on the same ground, we and they are like two pugilists who have been training in private quarters, and who have registered their prowess by the amount of punishment they have inflicted upon their sparring partners under the particular conditions which reign in each establishment.

As to the general effect of the new conditions, I think that the advent of America into the international ring will do more than merely make us strive harder; it should, and we all hope that it will, drive home to the Government the necessity for State recognition of racing – with particular regard to road racing – and for a certain amount of State encouragement which could be given in a number of ways in the building of British cars.

Has the word Brooklands ever passed the lips of a member of either House in anything louder than a whisper? Is not the phrase "road racing" taboo? Does not the general public still cling to the belief that all racing motorists are madmen intent, apparently, on no other purpose than breaking their necks? Is it possible for the man in the street to realize that there is just as much in taking cars round the track at 120 m.p.h. as there is in, say, some magnificent aeroplane achievement?

What a formidable questionnaire! What a revelation in a few sentences of the bias and ignorance which surrounds the whole business of motor racing!

In aeronautics we have few rivals, because the development of the aeroplane has been a national responsibility and the romance of it has caught hold of the public imagination like nothing else ever has or probably ever will do.

Had motor trials and motor racing received the blessing of the British Government at the outset, we should not now be faced with the everyday prospect of battling against long odds in the motoring arenas of the world and of having to meet the latest threat of "invasion" from America. Sooner or later the Government will realize that something will have to be done about it; in the meantime, private enterprise will continue the same discouraging struggle – under, I suppose, a sort of national frown.

The 1500-c.c. car is one of the brightest stars in our firmament, and I believe that we shall retain the useful lead we now hold, all credit to those – notably your own journal – who have vigorously fostered the type for so many years; but the 1½-litre limitation for international events will, as you have already pointed out, bring the invasion of America into the field of the light touring car very much closer. With that I am not at the moment intimately concerned, but I share the optimism which you have expressed as to the capability of Great Britain to hold her own in this particular sphere of activity, and I would cheerfully back a British producer against all comers.

Summed up, then, the situation from the racing point of view, which represents a standard of international comparison, is not at present very promising. America enters the field with an array of achievements already to her credit, many of which, when confirmed, will automatically annul those held by European concerns and regarded as of an international character; but time will tell, and judgement must not be passed until Europe has had time to adjust itself to the new conditions with which it is faced.

May I say, in conclusion, that, like the boxer who enters the ring, I am anxious to give Uncle Sam a hearty handshake – *and then get on with the business.*

J G Parry Thomas

Appendix B

Chronological table showing races in which Thomas was placed, and records taken.

F/S = flying start   S/S = standing start   F.T.D. = fastest time of day   W = world's record

Date 1922	Place	Car	Event	Result
21 May	Brooklands	Leyland	Essex M.C. Meeting	Earl of Athlone Lightning Handicap: 3rd
28 May	Laindon	Leyland	Essex County and Southend-on-Sea: A.C. Hill Climb	2nd, Class L 2nd and 4th, Class 4 2nd, Class 12 3rd, Class 18 Acceleration Test Class 1, equal 3rd
6 June	Brooklands	Leyland	B.A.R.C. Whit Monday Meeting	15th Lightning Short: 2nd 30th 100 m.p.h. Short: 1st 15th Lightning Long: 2nd 29th 100 m.p.h. Long: 2nd

Date	Location		Event	Results
16 June	Brooklands	Leyland	Records Class G	½ mile F/S 112·5 m.p.h. 1 kilo. F/S 111·62 m.p.h. 1 mile F/S 109·52 m.p.h. 2 miles F/S 108·69 m.p.h. 5 miles F/S 105·89 m.p.h. 10 miles F/S 105·62 m.p.h.
8 July	Holme Moss	Leyland	Bradford and Huddersfield Motor Clubs' Hill Climb	3rd, Class V
22 July	Brooklands	Leyland	Essex M.C. Meeting	Essex Lightning Long: 1st
7 Aug.	Brooklands	Leyland	B.A.R.C. August Meeting	16th Lightning Short: 2nd
2 Sept.	Brooklands	Leyland	S.E. Centre A.C.U. Meeting	Surrey Lightning Handicap: 1st (organised by Surbiton M.C.)
30 Sept.	Brooklands	Leyland	Essex M.C. Championship Meeting	1st in Heat Essex Senior Short: 1st Essex Senior Long: 3rd
14 Oct.	Brooklands	Leyland	B.A.R.C. Meeting	17th Lightning Short: 2nd 17th Lightning Long: 2nd 31st 100 m.p.h. Long: 3rd
16 Oct.	Brooklands	Leyland	Records Class G	1 mile F/S 110·08 m.p.h. 2 miles F/S 110·08 m.p.h.

Date	Venue	Event	Car	Results
9 Nov.	Brooklands	Records Class G	Leyland	5 miles F/S 110·08 m.p.h. 10 miles F/S 107·73 m.p.h. ½ mile F/S 119·05 m.p.h. 1 kilo. F/S 118·48 m.p.h. 1 mile F/S 116·77 m.p.h. 2 miles F/S 114·91 m.p.h. 5 miles F/S 115·06 m.p.h. 10 miles F/S 114·74 m.p.h. *W.*
11 Nov.	Brooklands	Armistice Day Meeting	Leyland	Lightning Handicap: 2nd
1923				
31 March	Brooklands	B.A.R.C. Easter Meeting	Leyland	18th Lightning Long: 2nd
19 May	Brooklands	B.A.R.C. Whitsun Meeting	Leyland	Brooklands Gold Vase: 1st
26 May	Laindon	Essex County and Southend A.C. Hill Climb	Leyland	Class N: 1st
2 June	Brooklands	Essex M.C. Meeting	Leyland	Essex Senior Short: 1st Essex Lightning Short: 1st Essex Lightning Long: 1st
20 June	Brooklands	Records Class G	Leyland	½ mile F/S 124·65 m.p.h. 1 Kilo. F/S 124·00 m.p.h.

Date	Location	Car	Event / Records	Result
23 June	Brooklands	Leyland	B.A.R.C. Summer Meeting	
28 June	Brooklands	Leyland	Records Class G	1 mile F/S 123·29 m.p.h.
				2 miles F/S 119·96 m.p.h.
				5 miles F/S 119·43 m.p.h. *W.*
				10 miles F/S 116·25 m.p.h. *W.*
30 June	Brooklands	Leyland	Surbiton M.C. Meeting	20th Lightning Long: 1st
				10 laps S/S 106·39 m.p.h.
				50 kms. S/S 176·78 m.p.h.
				Surrey Lightning Short: 5th
				Surrey Senior Lightning Long: 1st
				Surrey Junior Lightning Long: 1st
11 July	Brooklands	Leyland	Records Class G	200 miles 93·72 m.p.h.
				300 miles 91·46 m.p.h.
				400 miles 88·05 m.p.h.
				500 miles 87·08 m.p.h.
				600 miles 86·02 m.p.h.
				700 miles 86·27 m.p.h.
				2 hours 95·96 m.p.h.
				3 hours 91·23 m.p.h.

Date	Venue	Car	Event	Result
4 Aug.	Brooklands	Leyland	B.A.R.C. August Bank Holiday Meeting	4 hours 90·45 m.p.h. 5 hours 88·56 m.p.h. 6 hours 87·83 m.p.h. 7 hours 86·04 m.p.h. 8 hours 86·16 m.p.h. 9 hours 85·29 m.p.h. 21st Lightning Short: 2nd
3 Sept.	Brooklands	Leyland	Speed Trials	35th 100 m.p.h. Long: 2nd 1st (disqualified)
26 Sept.	Brooklands	Leyland	B.A.R.C. Meeting	22nd Lightning Short: 3rd 22nd Lightning Long: 2nd
29 Sept.	Brooklands	Leyland	Essex M.C. Meeting	Essex Lightning Long: 1st
1924				
21 April	Brooklands	Lanchester	B.A.R.C. Easter Meeting	38th 100 m.p.h. Short: 2nd (Lanchester)
3 May	Brooklands	4 cyl. Thomas Special	J.C.C. Meeting	13th 90 m.p.h. Short: 1st (Lanchester) Junior Long: 3rd

Date	Place	Car	Event	Results
22 May	Brooklands	Leyland-Thomas No. 1	Records Class G	1 kilo. F/S 124·12 m.p.h. 1 mile F/S 124·12 m.p.h. 2 miles F/S 124·12 m.p.h. 5 miles F/S 122·86 m.p.h. *W.* 10 miles F/S 120·46 m.p.h. *W.*
24 May	Brooklands	Leyland-Thomas No. 1	Ealing and District M.C. Meeting	3 lap Handicap: 3rd
27 May	Brooklands	Leyland-Thomas No. 1	Records Class G	50 kms. 179·31 k.p.h. *W.*
29 May	Brooklands	Leyland-Thomas No. 1	Records Class G	2 miles F/S 125·96 m.p.h. *W.*
9 June	Brooklands	Lanchester	B.A.R.C. Whitsun Meeting	38th 100 m.p.h. Long: 2nd
20 June	Skegness	Leyland-Thomas No. 1	Speed Trials	2nd F.T.D.
21 June	Saltburn	Leyland-Thomas No. 1	Speed Trials	3rd F.T.D.
26 June	Brooklands	Leyland-Thomas No. 1	Records Class G	½ mile F/S 134·33 m.p.h. 1 kilo. F/S 133·79 m.p.h. 1 mile F/S 131·48 m.p.h. (in one direction) 1 mile F/S 129·73 m.p.h. (both directions) *W.*
5 July	Brooklands	Leyland-Thomas No. 1	B.A.R.C. Midsummer Meeting	25th Lightning Short: 1st 25th Lightning Long: 1st

14 July	Brooklands	Leyland-Thomas No. 1	Records Class G	5 miles F/S 123·81 m.p.h. W. 10 kms. F/S 199·25 k.p.h.
19 July	Brooklands	Leyland-Thomas No. 1 Lanchester	Surbiton M.C. Meeting	Surrey Lightning Short: 1st (Leyland-Thomas) Surrey Junior Lightning Long: 1st (Lanchester)
21 July	Brooklands	Leyland-Thomas No. 1	Records Class G	100 kms. S/S 109·12 m.p.h. W. 50 kms. S/S 109·62 m.p.h.
23 July	Brooklands	Leyland-Thomas No. 1 Thomas Special (4 cyl.)	Essex M.C. Meeting	Essex Senior Short: 1st (Leyland-Thomas) Essex Senior Long: 2nd (Leyland-Thomas) Essex 30 miles Handicap: 1st (Thomas Special)
4 Aug.	Brooklands	Leyland-Thomas No. 1 Lanchester	B.A.R.C. August Meeting	26th Lightning Short: 2nd (Leyland-Thomas) 40th 100 m.p.h. Long: 2nd (Leyland-Thomas) 16th 90 m.p.h. Long: 3rd (Lanchester)

Date	Location	Car	Event	Results
7 Aug.	Brooklands	Lanchester	Records Class G	250 kms. 159·77 k.p.h.
				300 kms. 160·53 k.p.h.
				400 kms. 157·00 k.p.h.
				500 kms. 157·76 k.p.h.
				2 hours 104·08 m.p.h.
				3 hours 97·91 m.p.h.
				4 hours 98·34 m.p.h.
				200 miles –
				300 miles 97·95 m.p.h.
				400 miles 98·32 m.p.h.
27 Aug.	Boulogne	Leyland-Thomas No. 1	Speed Trials	F.T.D.
2 Sept.	Brooklands	Lanchester	Records Class G	12 hours 95·66 m.p.h. *W*.
				all Class G from 500 to 1000 miles
				700 to 1800 km.
				all Brooklands Class G records
13 Sept.	Brooklands	Leyland-Thomas No. 1	B.A.R.C. Autumn Meeting	42nd 100 m.p.h. Short: 2nd
				27th Lightning Short :1st
				41st 100 m.p.h. Long: 3rd
				27th Lightning Long: 1st

Date	Location	Car	Event	Result
4 & 5 Oct.	Montlhéry	Leyland-Thomas No. 1	Opening Meeting	6 lap race: 2nd fastest lap 131·89 m.p.h.
19 Oct.	Montlhéry	Leyland-Thomas No. 1	2nd Meeting	10 lap race: 1st
14 Nov.	Brooklands	Leyland-Thomas No. 1	Records Class G	50 miles 111·67 m.p.h. *W.* 50 kms. 180·54 k.p.h. *W.*
17 Nov.	Brooklands	Leyland-Thomas No. 1	Records Class G	1 hour 109·09 *W.* 100 miles 108·72 m.p.h. *W.* 150 kms. 174·88 k.p.h. *W.*
18 Nov.	Brooklands	Leyland-Thomas No. 1	Records Class G	200 kms. 172·81 k.p.h. *W.* 250 kms. 172·95 k.p.h. *W.* 150 miles 107·39 m.p.h. *W.*
19 Nov.	Brooklands	Leyland-Thomas No. 1	Records Class G	300 kms. 166·67 k.p.h. *W.* 200 miles 103·79 m.p.h. *W.* 2 hours 104·08 m.p.h. *W.*

1925

Date	Location	Car	Event	Result
25 April	Brooklands	Leyland-Thomas No. 1	Surbiton M.C. Meeting	Surbiton Junior Short: 4th (Thomas Special)
		4 Cyl. Thomas Special		Surrey lightning Long: 2nd (Leyland-Thomas)

Date	Location	Car	Event	Results
1 June	Brooklands	Leyland-Thomas No. -	B.A.R.C. Whitsun Meeting	Brooklands Gold Vase: 3rd Brooklands Founders' Gold Cup: 1st 42nd 100 m.p.h. Long: 3rd 28th Lightning Long: 1st
7 June	Montlhéry	Leyland-Thomas No. 1	Race Meeting	Race 9·3 miles: 2nd
15 June	Montlhéry	Leyland-Thomas No. 1	Records Class B	5 kms. 129·89 m.p.h. 5 miles 129·51 m.p.h. 10 kms. 129·24 m.p.h. 10 miles 122·89 m.p.h. W.
27 June	Brooklands	Leyland-Thomas No. 1 Lanchester	B.A.R.C. Summer Meeting	43rd 100 m.p.h. Long: 3rd (Leyland-Thomas) 20th 90 m.p.h. Long: 1st (Lanchester) 29th Lightning Long: 1st (Leyland-Thomas)
1 July	Brooklands	Leyland-Thomas No. 1	Records Class B	1 kilo. S/S 76·77 m.p.h. 1 mile S/S 88·26 m.p.h. 1 kilo. F/S 132·99 m.p.h. 1 mile F/S 132·30 m.p.h.

Date	Location	Car	Event	Result
2 July	Brooklands	Leyland-Thomas No. 1	Records Class B	5 kms. F/S 124·83 m.p.h.
				5 miles F/S 124·08 m.p.h.
				10 kms. F/S 123·56 m.p.h.
				10 miles F/S 122·31 m.p.h.
11 July	Brooklands	Leyland-Thomas No. 1	West Kent Club Meeting	50 kms. 113·82 m.p.h. *W.*
				50 miles 114·60 m.p.h. *W.*
				100 kms. 114·63 m.p.h. *W.*
14 July	Brooklands	Leyland-Thomas No. 1	Records class B	Match with Eldridge: 1st
				1 hour 110·64 m.p.h. *W.*
				100 miles 110·47 m.p.h. *W.*
1925				
1 Aug.	Brooklands	Leyland-Thomas No. 1	B.A.R.C. August Meeting	35th 75 m.p.h. Short: 4th
		4 cyl. Thomas Special		(Thomas Special)
				35th 75 m.p.h. Long: 1st
				(Thomas Special)
		Lanchester		44th 100 m.p.h. Long:
				1st (Lanchester)
				30th Lightning Long:

Date	Venue	Car	Event	Result
17 Aug.	Brooklands	4 cyl. Thomas Special	Records Class E	2nd (Leyland-Thomas) 100 miles Handicap: 1st (Thomas Special) 1 kilo. S/S 104·167 k.p.h. 1 mile S/S 72·86 m.p.h.
12 Sept.	Brooklands	Lanchester	B.A.R.C. Autumn Meeting	45th 100 m.p.h. Long: 2nd
1926				
4 April	Brooklands	Lanchester	B.A.R.C. Easter Meeting	46th 100 m.p.h. Long: 1st
27 April	Pendine	"Babs"	Records World's	1 kilo. F/S 169·238 m.p.h. *W.* 1 mile F/S 168·074 m.p.h. *W.*
28 April	Pendine	"Babs"	Records World's	1 kilo. F/S 171·09 m.p.h. *W.* 1 mile F/S 170·624 m.p.h. *W.*
24 May	Brooklands	"Babs"	B.A.R.C. Whitsun Meeting	33rd Lightning Long: 2nd ("Babs")
		Leyland-Thomas No. –		*The Star* Gold Star Handicap: 2nd (Leyland-Thomas)
8 June	Brooklands	Leyland-Thomas No. –	Records Class B	5 miles 126·35 m.p.h. 10 kms. 126·26 m.p.h. 10 miles 126·03 m.p.h. *W.*

Date	Venue	Car	Meeting	Result
15 June	Brooklands	Leyland-Thomas No. 1	Records Class B	1 kilo. S/S 77.35 m.p.h. 1 mile S/S 88·47 m.p.h.
2 July	Brooklands	Lanchester	B.A.R.C. Summer Meeting	24th 90 m.p.h. Long: 1st
31 July	Brooklands	"Babs"	August Meeting	35th Lightning Short: 2nd ("Babs")
		Leyland-Thomas No. 1		49th 100 m.p.h. Long: 1st (Leyland-Thomas) 35th Lightning Long: 1st (Leyland-Thomas)
		Vauxhall		Evening News 100 miles' Handicap: 3rd (Vauxhall)
14 Aug.	Brooklands	Leyland-Thomas No. 1	Essex M.C. Meeting	Essex Lightning Long: 2nd Winners' Handicap: 2nd Cars v. Motor Cycles: 3rd
11 Sept.	Brooklands	Leyland-Thomas No. 1	B.A.R.C. Autumn Meeting	36th Lightning Short: 1st (Leyland-Thomas) 50th 100 m.p.h. Long: 3rd (Lanchester) 36th Lightning Long: 1st (Leyland-Thomas)
		Lanchester		

Date	Location	Car	Event	Result
25 Sept.	Brooklands	8 cyl. Thomas Special	200 Miles Race	8th
2 Oct.	Brooklands	Leyland-Thomas No. 1	Essex M.C. Meeting	Essex Senior Long: 1st (Leyland-Thomas)
	Brooklands	8 cyl. Thomas Special		Essex 50 miles Handicap: 1st (Thomas Special)
7 Oct.	Brooklands	Leyland-Thomas No. 1	Records Class B	500 kms. 179·027 k.p.h. *W.* 1000 kms. 176·655 k.p.h. 500 miles 110·04 m.p.h. *W.* 3 hours 111·28 m.p.h. *W.* 6 hours 109·96 m.p.h.
14 Oct.	Brooklands	"Babs"	Records Class A	5 miles 124·25 m.p.h. 10 miles 122·91 m.p.h. 10 kms. 123·91 m.p.h.
21 Oct.	Brooklands	Leyland-Thomas No. 1	Records Class B	1 hour 121·74 m.p.h. *W.* 100 kms. 111·67 m.p.h.
30 Oct.	Brooklands	8 cyl. Thomas Special	Records Class F	100 miles 112·60 m.p.h. 1 hour 112·77 m.p.h.

Index

177